Government

★ ★ ★ ★ ★ ★

JJ DeSpain and Phyllis Schomaker

Publications International, Ltd.

JJ DeSpain writes for major national magazines in the United States and Canada. Her special areas of interest include health, consumer advice, and family issues. She has had a variety of experiences working with and for government groups, including the Veterans Administration.

Phyllis Schomaker has had a decade-long career in library science, most recently working at a government depository library. Writing projects include her book *Household Forms to Save Time and Simplify Your Life*.

CONTENTS

★ ★ ★ ★

GOVERNMENT SECRETS
An Introduction

★ ★ ★ ★

THE MAJORITY of the American public believes their government keeps the truth from them. It does.

When confronted, officials usually give "national security" as the reason for this secrecy. Often, secrecy is really about protecting certain individuals. Almost every night on the TV news, we hear stories about some government official or agency that has been hiding something. It makes you wonder just how many secrets there are. Well, here is a book full of them!

Eighty percent of Americans believe the government is hiding knowledge about extraterrestrial life forms. Did you know that defense contractors billed the government more than $20,000 for golf balls? There are "active" FBI files on people who have been dead for decades. New York prisoners sued the government because they had been given bad haircuts.

Not all the information in this book concerns swindlers and prisoners. For instance, you will learn that anybody can take advantage of government surplus auctions without paying for expensive kits or instructional videos. The government is happy to tell you how to do it *for free*. After all, they're the ones who want to get rid of the stuff! Don't pay some infomercial guru when you can just call an 800 number or go to the Internet and click your way to a government Web site.

Government Secrets is the result of extensive research into what our government is really doing in the areas of medical research, benefits for its citizens, free giveaways and information for the asking, secret studies, and scandalous spending. There are only two big differences between the official reports (where the facts are hidden) and this book. *Government Secrets* is written in everyday plain English—and it's not dull.

Ours is an independent society, and we should be able to learn anything we want to know by simply looking in the right places. Of course, this is a double-edged sword: You, too, can be found out. How much do you want your boss or neighbor to know about you? Is anything too personal?

You want to know how your congressperson voted on the important issues. Do you also need to know where he or she buys underwear? You want to know about a convicted child molester moving into your area. But do you have a right to know how much your next-door neighbor pays in alimony? Read on to learn what is and what is not accessible to the public.

Discover hundreds of little-known details about the workings of your government—the good, the bad, and the ugly. Learn how your tax dollars are being spent—and about the tax shelters that make everyone else's taxes higher.

Our government is an open book. Anyone can check it out of the "library"—if they know how. Reading *Government Secrets* will show you how to deal with the government and how to keep track of your dealings.

And for those of you who *really* want to know where your congressperson buys underwear, you can learn how to find that out, too.

WHAT THE GOVERNMENT KNOWS ABOUT YOU

And How to Keep It (Relatively) Secret

★ ★ ★ ★

WHEN YOU CALL the local pizza delivery place, the dispatcher on the other end of the line knows your name and address, the shortest route to your house, and your most recent pizza preferences even before you order. That might be a bit unnerving, but it's nothing compared to how we have lost control of the terms under which personal information is acquired, disclosed, and used through accessing government agencies. Here's what's going on and how to keep your information safe.

YOU ARE 1,000,000 STATISTICS

Are you aware of the hundreds of thousands of personal records about your life stored in huge government information systems and databases? Knowing who has access to this knowledge can help you safeguard your personal identity and protect yourself from unscrupulous people. Financial loss, destruction of your credit rating, and even loss of your reputation are all possible in today's digital society.

Every event in your life, from birth to death—

including buying a house or car, starting a new job, applying for a loan, even getting a dog license—creates a paper trail of your personal history. You may think that no one but you has access to these records and that no harm can come from someone finding out your mother's maiden name. Yet banks always ask for that very information to verify your identity when you try to conduct business by telephone. Let's examine exactly what government agencies (federal, state, and local) have on you, who can access that data, and what can be done with it.

BEWARE OF PUBLICLY ACCESSIBLE GOVERNMENT RECORDS

A thief with fraudulent aims, armed only with a Social Security Number (SSN), can completely steal someone's identity and destroy that person's finances, credit, and reputation. Given that someone with these intentions would have no qualms about falsifying a few documents, telling a few lies, or even forging a signature or two, such a person could use a SSN and some other documents to get a driver's license in almost any state. With a good story to explain the change in address, he or she could also obtain credit or take out loans in your name. The misfortunes like those shown below could easily be your own.

- For four long years, Bronti Kelly could not get or keep a job. He eventually learned that a man arrested for shoplifting and other crimes had been using his stolen identity, and the information showed up in employers' background checks.

- William Dwyer, an aerospace engineer for NASA, had his credit information stolen and sold to a Nigerian crime ring. Over a period of four years, his name and his wife's were used to rack up $35,000 worth of charges through 42 different credit card accounts.

HOW EASY IS IT TO ACCESS GOVERNMENT RECORDS?

Most of the databases and confidential files that contain sensitive information about individual citizens are not supposed to be available for public access. However, most are easily available to anyone acting in an official capacity relative to a civil or criminal court case. This includes private investigators. And guess what? Almost *anyone* can get a P.I. license. If you happen to live in one of the states that does impose a few obstacles, it's usually easy enough to overcome them. Twelve states have absolutely no requirements for licensing, and only in nine states can you be disqualified from becoming a P.I. if you have been convicted of a felony.

But why bother even going through *that* much work?

Plenty of info is accessible over the Internet to anyone for little or no cost. Take a look at the following list of investigative tools available on just one Web site:

- Reverse phone number search. Have a phone number and wonder who it belongs to? You can find out here.

- Reverse address search. Use any U.S. street address to find the name and phone number of the occupant.

- Telephone directory search. Search millions of listings around the world for the address or phone number you need.

- Social Security Number verification. Type in any SSN and find out when and where it was issued.

- Social Security Death Index search. Input an individual's name and state to learn when they died.

- Name/address change search. Did someone

change their name or mailing address? Get their new information here.

- U.S. Armed Forces Personnel search, by Military City Online. This allows you to locate active-duty military personnel. (This list requires that you subscribe.)

- Physician Board certification. Verify that your doctor is board-certified and in what areas.

- Database descriptions. This gives explanations of many popular database searches used by private investigators, as well as what information is required for each search and what you can expect to get back.

- Links to other resources. Here you can find additional sources of information, from Forensics to the FBI.

For $25, another site will sell you the computer application necessary to set up your own investigative agency via your personal computer. Their advertising makes it seem as if snooping and sleuthing would make ideal hobbies:

"Find out EVERYTHING you ever wanted to know about your friends, family, neighbors, employees, even your boss." "Get a copy of your FBI file." "Check DRIVING and CRIMINAL RECORDS." "FIND DEBTORS and locate HIDDEN ASSETS." "Find out how much ALIMONY your neighbor is paying."

In case you don't feel confident about your computer skills, another commercial Web site offers to do the work for you—for a fee. Here is a sample of their products:

- A "level one" package searches one credit bureau as well as other sources, includes the subject's name; SSNs used; address history; neighbors' names, addresses, and phone numbers; bankruptcy check; judgments found;

lien check; real property ownership records; owners of place of current residence; corporate involvements; UCC filings (business loans); aircraft owned; and vessels owned. This costs $39.

- The "level two" package ($59) searches ALL major credit bureaus and includes all of the above, plus any aliases used and names, addresses, and phone numbers of relatives.

- A "level three" background check will include all the above information, as well as vehicle registrations, driver's license information, and the names of all other persons who have shared the same address as the subject. This costs $99.

- Include an extra $39 with any of the above searches and you can add a regional asset/civil search for that person, retrieving detailed information on sources and figures.

These companies accept payment by check and credit card and require you to fill out a form of identifying information about yourself. All information is guaranteed to be kept confidential. (And if you can't trust an information broker with *your* information, who *can* you trust?)

WHO HAS PUBLIC RECORDS OF YOU?

- Social Security Administration: It knows where nearly everybody is and even what name everyone operates under. These files contain a record of every job you ever held, even part-time jobs you worked as a kid; your home addresses for every place you ever lived while holding a job; the amount of money you made; the number of dependents you claimed; and the amount of taxes you paid.

- FBI: It has virtually unlimited power to confiscate all personal records, including financial and bank statements, phone call histories, and even lists of your checked-out library books and video rentals. The FBI is performing massive monitoring of ordinary citizens through video security systems and telephone monitoring networks. Such prying seems justified when the FBI tracks down the Oklahoma City bomber by video-surveillance, truck rental records, motel registers, and feed store receipts. But it has to make you uncomfortable to think that your *own* lawn fertilizer purchases are also fair game.

- CIA: The truth is out there, and they have ways to find it. Their methods are so sophisticated that even electronic equipment often cannot detect their snooping. They can trace the location of anyone using a mobile phone—even if it's turned off. And they can track anyone's credit card usage (on the pretext of catching criminals) with no need for proof, evidence, or results.

- IRS: Their files hold not only

TOP SECRET

THE SPY WHO ROBBED ME

A former U.S. diplomat suspected of espionage while working at the U.S. Embassy in Vienna in 1989 was recently arrested and charged with stealing $100 worth of groceries from a store in Chapel Hill, NC. Two store employees said they saw the former government agent (who took a job bagging at the supermarket after being canned by the State Department) cart away unpaid-for groceries in his Mercedes-Benz.

your personal and business income tax returns themselves, but also massive studies and reports used to make projections and help the government plan fiscal policies. Some people think the purpose of these policies is to maintain the economic status quo.

- Military and Veterans Administration: These records contain the past and present home addresses, names and ages of dependents, service records, benefits paid, health and hospitalization files, and salary grades for the lifetime of more than five million men and women who have served in any branch of the armed services.

- DMV (Department of Motor Vehicles): This agency maintains driver's license records, motor vehicle registrations, and traffic violations, as well as all personal information contained on the applications for licenses and

TOP SECRET

WHERE'S THE MONEY GOING?

The Environmental Protection Agency, asked to officially respond to a congressional report charging that the agency used too many outside contractors, paid an outside contractor $20,000 to write a response! Total federal low-income programs to the poor cost the average taxpayer about $400 annually—while the safety net for *private corporations* costs the average taxpayer around $1,400! The federal government spends roughly $75 million a year to subsidize private businesses.

registrations (like your SSN, date of birth, limitations, and physical description).

- Voter Registration: These records yield many personal details, such as your name, address, SSN, date and state of birth, occupation, unlisted phone numbers, names of other people living at the same address, and even copies of your actual signature.

- U.S. District Court Records: The court files decisions and official records connected with both civil and criminal cases as well as those of bankruptcy and naturalization proceedings.

- Recorder's Office: It keeps a permanent record of all documents affecting land transfers, including names in grantor/grantee index trusts, quit-claims, mechanics' and tax liens, powers of attorney, judgments, and sometimes even copies of death certificates.

- Assessor's Office: It keeps a register of all properties countywide and a list of where tax bills for those properties are sent. These documents give site locations, legal descriptions, assessed values, structure summaries, and the names and addresses of the taxpayers.

- Vital Statistics: This office keeps birth, death, and marriage records for each county. Each type of record contains varying types of information on parents, such as their address, occupations, birthplaces, race, SSNs, dates of birth, years of education, number of prior marriages, etc.

- County Clerk/Superior Court Index: This office holds the actual case files of civil suits, which include money disputes, probate filings, divorces, harassment charges, restraining orders, and appeals from municipal and small claims courts.

Attorneys' names and legal actions are included, as well as statements by process servers that even show where the party was served. Criminal cases held in municipal courts—even murder and man-slaughter as well as shoplifting, embezzlement, theft, burglary, assault, drug peddling, drug possession, and bad check charges—are all included within this domain.

FOUR WAYS TO PROTECT YOURSELF

1. Shred or destroy ALL of the old records that you intend to toss into the trash.

2. *Never* give your SSN to anyone you don't know—especially over the telephone.

3. The national credit bureaus offer a toll-free number that enables customers to opt out of all pre-approved credit offers with just one phone call (888-5-OPTOUT). This will at least keep credit card offers with your name and address from finding their way into mailboxes.

4. Ask creditors and banks what happens to the information you provide. Many will allow you to opt out of having your information shared with other agencies. This will help limit the accessibility of your personal data.

We live in a free and open society. Given the alternatives, want to keep it that way. We can use the information age to our advantage. We can be sure that the people with whom we deal are who they say they are. We can watchdog government officials. We can make informed decisions. However, with all privileges come responsibility. Ours must be to safeguard our identities, our credit histories, and our private information by making sure that our personal histories are accurate—and not misused.

Tax Loopholes and Financial Finds

From Uncle Sam to You

★ ★ ★ ★

TRY TO THINK OF TAXES as a game that you can learn to play—and win. One big way to win at taxes is to develop a whole new attitude toward doing them in the first place. Many of the best tax savings have been around for years, yet are still underused. More people than you would think overpay because they don't take advantage of legitimate tax breaks. The following "tricks of the trade" are not really secrets but facts buried within the tax laws that most people fail to look at—just because they hate dealing with taxes.

HELP FOR THE HELPERS

According to the U.S. Census Bureau, 3.9 million American children are raised primarily by a grandparent. More than one million children have no parent contributing to their welfare at all.

Uncle Sam thinks people in this situation need a break. You may be able to claim extra dependents, write off certain kinds of cash gifts (if documented properly), or even take the earned income credit, one of the biggest tax breaks in years for middle-income Americans.

Stipends earned by foster parents or foster grandparents are considered non-taxable income anyway, since they usually do not cover more than basic expenses. But the earned income credit can provide a really great tax break for those who help others. In 1998, the IRS initiated a $400 per child tax credit that applies to a qualifying dependent child, grandchild, stepchild, foster child, or adoptee. The child must be a U.S. citizen or resident and be younger than 17.

HELP FOR HOMEOWNERS

Your home is your castle and an asset around tax time. Be sure to keep all receipts for repairs and improvements, and make sure you're aware of the following sale and loan deductions.

When you've sold your home, you can deduct improvements that can lower taxable profits, including anything that has a useful life of a year or more (new

IRS MYTHS

Myth #1: *Confessions to your tax advisor are confidential.* This is not so. Confidentiality is only assured if the advisor is also an attorney.

Myth #2: *Extensions trigger audits.* There is no connection between the two.

Myth #3: *Peel-off labels trigger audits.* On the contrary; they speed up processing.

Myth #4: *Once your refund is in hand, you won't get audited.* Actually, you are fair game for three years.

Myth #5: *It's good to spend more money in order to get more deductions.* It's actually not worth it.

Myth #6: *Losses from the sale of a home are deductible.* Not so.

plumbing, wiring, paving, basement refinishing, a new fence or roof). Many things taken for granted as normal upkeep are forgotten when it comes time to pay taxes on the profit from the sale of a house.

Exclusion of the profits up to $250,000 from the sale of your main home are also deductible. At one time this was a once-in-a-lifetime benefit, but it is now available as often as every two years.

Home equity interest is deductible. The interest on debt from a home equity loan is also deductible, even if you used the proceeds for personal expenditures. It could be to your advantage to pay off a large credit card debt with a home equity loan. Credit card interest rates can be as high as 21 percent and are not tax deductible.

TOP SECRET

WORKING FOR SOMEBODY ELSE

Tax Freedom Day, the day each year when Americans stop working to pay taxes and begin working solely for themselves, gets later all the time. In 1950, it came April 3. In 1998, it fell on May 10.... The average family in 1998 worked two hours and 50 minutes of each eight-hour day to pay taxes, with an hour and 55 minutes going solely for federal taxes. The average household now pays $9,445 in federal income taxes—*twice* the 1985 total.

OVERLOOKED MEDICAL DEDUCTIONS

Watching out for these deductions can save you money!

- Any special treatment or equipment you receive on the advice of a doctor is deductible! At times, deductions have been permitted for saunas, whirlpools, and occasionally even swimming pools—at least to the extent that their cost exceeds the increased value of your property.

- Mileage for trips to the doctor in your car are deductible at the rate of ten cents per mile.

- Medical expenses not performed by, but recommended by, your doctor are *completely* deductible. These include back or neck massage, acupuncture, herbal treatments, vitamin therapy, and the like.

- The cost of having a pet can be a legitimate health expense. Although medical research shows that pets are beneficial for all of us, this alone may not be enough for the deduction. It is best to have a written recommendation

(which is not difficult to get) from your doctor. Animals are now providing therapeutic assistance to patients with epilepsy, seizures, certain heart and blood pressure problems, and even diabetes.

OVERLOOKED SMALL BUSINESS DEDUCTIONS

Check those work expenses and benefit from them.

- Prescription eyeglasses used for your business are deductible. Eyeglasses often need special customization for use with a computer or to do fine craft work. Have the optometrist write "for occupational use only" on the prescription, and it becomes a business deduction.

- Take the home office deduction. The IRS is now

HOW BIG IS THE TAX CODE?

The total tax law consists of 101,295 pages, or 7.05 million words. In contrast, the Bible has "just" 1,291 pages, or 774,746 words.

How Tax Returns Are Chosen for Review

- **Computer scoring:** A computer program called the Discriminant Function System (DiF) numerically scores returns after processing and identifies returns most likely to need review.

- **Large corporations:** The IRS examines some large corporate returns annually as part of its large case and Coordinated Examination Program (CEP).

- **Information matching:** Returns are examined when information from W-2s and interest statements do not agree with income reported on the return.

- **Related examinations:** Returns may be selected for audit when they involve issues or transactions with other taxpayers whose returns were selected for audit.

- **District offices may also identify returns in connection with any local compliance initiative.**

less picky about this than in the past. Retirement is an excellent time to start up a small business, either in the area of a lifetime of expertise or in a totally new direction (such as a much-loved hobby or aspiration). You can deduct portions of your utilities, rent, phone bills, and other business expenses. You can hire your children or grandchildren and help them earn cash while lowering your taxes at the same time. You can also purchase your supplies wholesale and write them off your taxable income. If your business *doesn't* make a profit, you can use the losses to offset other income for three out of five years.

- Remember those business lunches. If you take a friend to lunch, and they are a *possible* business prospect or networking contact, that lunch is deductible.

- Take mileage for business consulting. Many retired people offer their expertise on either a paid or voluntary basis. Either way, transportation expense is deductible.

PENALTY-FREE IRA WITHDRAWALS

You may now avoid the ten percent penalty for withdrawing funds from your IRA account before age 59½ if you use the funds for the following:

- First-time home buying. A surviving spouse may qualify as a first-time home buyer if the previous homes were held in joint ownership. This could be a great way to buy a little retirement cottage or a condominium in a senior community.

TOP SECRET

MOOOOOD MUSIC

Researchers at Purdue University, funded by a half-million-dollar U.S. Department of Agriculture grant to study the moods of livestock, report that dairy cows do not like the music made by the rock group Kiss, but they do like Mozart. Scientists say that such research on cows, as well as on chickens and pigs, is very important to the U.S. economy. Why? Because happy cows produce more milk than grumpy cows.

- Education expenses. Now that the children are raised, it might be a good time to think about that degree you wish you had gotten.

- Medical expenses or medical insurance premiums after losing your job. Many older workers are downsized before collecting retirement benefits.

Filing Help for Seniors

The IRS provides more than 11,000 Tax Counseling for the Elderly sites. These volunteer programs are set up in shopping centers, libraries, churches, or community centers. The sites are advertised each year in local newspapers.

Lifetime Learning Credit

The government will pay up to $1,000 of tuition and education expenses for any student, regardless of age, enrolled in college after June 30, 1998. It will even cover graduate-level classes, for which it is very difficult to find financial aid.

The Hope Credit

You can claim a tax credit of up to $1,500 per eligible student (including yourself) for the first two years of college. This can include costs of tuition, enrollment, supplies, and equipment. The credit requires at least half-time student status, which amounts to two courses per semester.

But Be Careful ...

Be careful about your choices, however, because the Hope Credit and the Lifetime Learning Credit may *not* be taken in the same year.

Student Loan Interest

Up to $1,000 of student loan interest is deductible without needing to itemize deductions to get the credit. It comes right off the 1040 or 1040A. This is to help supplement the educational benefits already offered by the government.

Capital Gains News

The 18-month capital gains holding period has been

More Tax Cheats in Jail

Ten years ago, over half of those convicted of tax offenses received probation. Last year, 70 percent of those convicted of criminal tax offenses (over 21,000 people) were sentenced to jail or home detention.

eliminated. This means that any assets held for less than one year before being sold are taxed at the short-term rate (i.e., the ordinary income rate), which is now the same as the long-term rates of 10 to 20 percent, depending on your tax bracket.

Investment Costs

Miscellaneous deductions are subject to the two percent limit, so don't overlook some of the things that can help bump you over that limit. *All* expenses of producing income are deductible. This means you can deduct depreciation on your home computer if you use it to manage your investments. You can deduct subscriptions to publications that help you produce income. You can deduct fees you pay to a broker, bank, or trustee to collect investment income. However, keep in mind that you cannot deduct a fee to a broker to buy investment property, such as stocks and bonds.

Job Search Deductions

If you've lost your job to downsizing, you can deduct the cost of sending out résumés and getting interviews—even if you take early retirement or branch out on your own. Why would you do that? Well, you can make contacts, do

---

How to Get Your Refund FASTER!

- Use preprinted address labels. They include the bar coding the IRS computer can read. Otherwise, someone has to key in your information.
- Use the bar-coded envelope provided.
- Put your forms in correct sequence according to the number in the upper right-hand corner of each form.
- Double check that you have signed the forms and that you have not left any blank spaces.
- File early.

TOTAL PAPER IRS RETURNS PROJECTED FOR 1999

Form 1040 is the most used form (61.4 million users).

Form 1040A is expected to be used by 14.5 million.

Form 1040EZ: 11.4 million.

Form 1040PC: 8.7 million.

The total number of paper forms expected in 1999 is 96 million.

important networking, and keep in touch with your field, all while giving yourself a nice tax deduction.

THE FRIENDLY IRS

If you overpay on your taxes, don't worry—you'll get your money back. Should the IRS discover an error in your favor, you will receive a check, along with complete explanations of your errors and their corrections. (Could it be that the IRS is our friend after all?) Not even a friendly IRS, however, can help you with information that it does not have. Only *you* know about deductions you can take, and a tax specialist can only work with the information you have provided.

BRING ON THE STORMS!

If you live in a zip code of a federally declared national disaster area, you will be forgiven interest and penalties for filing your federal taxes late. In California alone, nearly 700,000 taxpayers have gotten back at least $25 million. And the government really means business: If you send in the payment anyway, they will send it back. You never know when there might be a little windfall coming your way.

HIDDEN ENTITLEMENT FACT

The IRS says that prior to the 1986 Tax Reform Act, one of every ten people making more than $200,000 who paid no federal income tax at all claimed charitable donations of more than 30 percent of their income.

HIDDEN MEDICAL INFORMATION
Secrets to Keep You Healthy

★ ★ ★ ★

CHRONIC CONDITIONS ASSOCIATED WITH AGING significantly limit daily activity for 39 percent of persons over age 65. And that doesn't just concern older folks; it concerns everyone. We all grow older if we're lucky. The National Institute of Health, the Administration on Aging, and several government organizations and federally funded programs have joined efforts to help our nation's senior citizens take on the aging process.

FALLS

Every year, one of every three people over age 65 falls. According to the *Annual Review of Public Health,* more than 7,700 people died in 1995 as a result of falls. For people over age 85, they are the leading cause of injury-related death. For those 65 and over, 60 percent of all fatal falls occur in the home, 30 percent in public places, and ten percent in health care institutions.

The CDC (Centers for Disease Control), NFPA (National Fire Protection Association), A.A. (Administration on Aging), and other agencies have collaborated on research projects to help reduce falls and injuries from falls among the elderly. Take note of these recommendations:

- Increased physical activity to improve strength, mobility, and flexibility.

- New strategies to provide adequate supervision.

- Minimal use of psychoactive medications.

- Environmental modifications, such as grab bars and railings and the removal of trip hazards like uneven floors, slippery surfaces, poor lighting, and unstable furniture.

FRACTURES

Never ignore a pain in the butt. Most of them are almost impossible to dismiss, and that's a good thing. Pain in the groin or buttocks can be a sign of bone death. It's called hip osteonecrosis, and it causes 180,000 Americans each year to undergo hip replacement surgery, a very difficult procedure with often severe complications and a painful recovery. Doctors are working on a better and more permanent cure.

In 1998, thirteen patients underwent an experimental procedure called osteoregeneration. All thirteen surgeries have proven successful. Doctors implant a capsule into a hole drilled into the end of the thigh bone. The capsule is filled with a protein that stimulates bone growth; the adjoining bone is coated with an implant of cadaver bone coated with the same protein. Growth of new bone prevents further osteoarthritis in the treated hip.

The NIH supports an organization called the Osteoporosis and related Bone Diseases National Resource Center. Get info at the Osteogenesis Imperfecta Foundation's Web site: www.oif.org.

STROKE AND HEART DISEASE

Did you know that depression may actually be a sign of stroke? In a recent study of more than 200 patients suffering from moderate depression, mini-strokes, undetectable because they did not produce typical symptoms such as paralysis, were revealed as the actual cause. Researchers believe that this "vascular depression" could account for as much as 30 to 40 percent of all depression in people over age 65.

These findings warrant further examination, especially for anyone with a family history of heart disease, diabetes, high blood pressure, or clogged arteries. Depression is a possible symptom of a more serious medical problem.

Find tips for avoiding strokes at the National Institute of Neurological Disorders and Stroke Web site: www.ninds.nih.gov/patients/disorder.

TOP SECRET

READY OR NOT, HERE COMES 2000

Y2K computer problems could potentially affect gas, power, and phone services, transportation, government agencies, financial services, and import/export businesses. But a new phone service (888-USA-4Y2K) offers free information in common areas of Y2K concern. Information comes from primary sources including government agencies, companies, and industry groups.

ARTHRITIS AND OSTEOPOROSIS

The FDA recently approved a new once-a-day medicine, Vioxx, for pain relief in osteoarthritis. Scientists believe that this new drug blocks the enzyme that triggers pain and inflammation while sparing a related enzyme that helps maintain the normal stomach lining. Although the new drug has encouraging results, many people cannot take it because of adverse side effects or allergies.

Raloxifene, a new drug, is showing promise in reducing bone loss due to osteoporosis. It increases bone density much as estrogen therapy does without stimulating endometrial tissue (possibly a risk for causing cancer).

Acupuncture: Many Americans are still skeptical about the benefits of the ancient Chinese therapy that uses thin, sharp needles to redirect a life energy known as *chi*. But recent research has shown that much of the pain from arthritis in the knees has been relieved for up to 12 weeks by this treatment when accompanied by anti-inflammatory medication. According to Dr. Bryan Berman, director of the Division of Complementary Medicine at Kernan Hospital in Baltimore, "acupuncture was indeed helpful for osteoarthritis of the knees."

Medicare does not yet pay for acupuncture, but a bipartisan group of house reps introduced a bill in 1999 to expand the types of services patients can use to relieve pain—including acupuncture—without having to endure a long and often fruitless FDA approval process.

MEDICAL MONEY FACTS

- Hip fractures account for more than $3 billion in medical costs each year.

- According to recent CDC (Centers for Disease Control) statistics, older Americans make up 13 percent of the population but account for nearly 36 percent of health care costs.

- Sixty million people will have arthritis by the year 2020, at an estimated annual cost of $65 billion.

Pain Problems

Research shows that older people have a higher threshold for pain than younger people! Prevalence of pain increases from early adulthood until approximately age 60. It seems to then reach a plateau and may decline in extreme old age. This means that even mild pain can indicate a serious problem in an older patient.

The problem is that our medical care system typically considers mild-to-moderate pain in the elderly to be inevitable. Health care professionals are often reluctant to refer older patients to pain clinics, yet one study shows that such clinics offer significant improvements in 95 percent of their older patients. The lesson here is that seniors should refuse to accept pain as something they have to "live with" and instead demand that their doctors provide methods to *deal* with it.

The Osteogenesis Imperfecta Foundation deals with general pain management questions at www.oif.org/tier2/pain.htm.

Chronic Fatigue

Another common complaint, often accepted as a fact of life for older people, is tiredness. However, there are effective solutions for many conditions that cause serious fatigue. The first step is to evaluate the symptoms associated with weariness. A detailed discussion with a doctor should help to determine if there is an underlying cause, such as:

- depression
- anemia
- hypothyroidism
- menopause
- allergies
- sleep apnea
- chronic fatigue syndrome

The treatments for these conditions should help alleviate the symptoms of tiredness. In addition, doctors are finding that fatigue problems can be reduced or eliminated by proper nutrition; vitamins and herbs; stress reduction; application of light, water, and sound stimulation; breathing exercises; physical activity; yoga; acupressure; and some new prescription drugs.

NUTRIENTS FOR THE EYES

Fifty million people are blind because of cataracts. More than a half-million cataract operations are performed each year in the United States. Doctors now believe that proper nutrition should prevent more than half of these surgeries. Even with the latest surgical techniques, which promise no needles, patches, stitches and instant recovery, it's still better to prevent cataracts if possible. High levels of the

CHOLESTEROL-LOWERING AIDS

- Soluble fiber found in oat bran, some beans, baked potatoes with skin, oranges, and psyllium (also found in Metamucil).

- Garlic. Eating half a clove a day has been shown to decrease cholesterol levels by nine percent.

- Soy.

- Nicotonic acid (niacin), which also ups "good" cholesterol.

- Bile-acid resins such as cholestyramine (available as Questran or in generic form).

- Cholestin (Chinese red yeast), sold over the counter at health food stores, contains lovastatin—which is also found in Mevacor. Remember that Cholestin is a drug and should be taken only under a doctor's supervision.

- Fibrates such as gemfibrozil and fenofibrate are lipid-modifying agents. They also raise "good" cholesterol by 10–15 percent.

- The government has information to help you lower your cholesterol. Go to http://rover.nhlbi.nih.gov/cgi-bin/chl/how.cgi and to http://rover.nhlbi.nih.gov/chl/faqall.htm.

antioxidants vitamin C, beta carotene, vitamin E, and selenium have all been found to prevent or delay cataract formation.

DEPRESSION

Is this treatment for the birds? Actually, no. A new program called the Eden Alternative introduces gardens and animals into the nursing home setting. The effects have been so dramatic that many new studies have been initiated on the healing power of animals with depressed older patients.

Dr. John Morley, gerontologist at St. Louis University Medical Center, notes that people who spent all their time in their rooms started interacting as soon as animals arrived. A key factor in the experiment is to make the patients responsible for the care of both animals and plants. It's difficult to feel useless when something depends on you, and nearly impossible to feel lonely when something adores you the way that only a devoted pet can.

Meanwhile, nonaddictive medications with fewer side effects constantly come on the market after FDA screening. Most of them, such as Prozac, are in the serotonin reuptake inhibitor family. However, before using *any* drug, be sure to have a complete physical examination to eliminate any physical problems that could be causing depression.

ALZHEIMER'S DISEASE

Tropicamide, a fluid used by ophthalmologists in eye examinations, may prove to be the most accurate test yet for diagnosing Alzheimer's disease. This simple test could eventually replace the difficult, costly, and often inconclusive ones currently available. Government and industry tests are still being undertaken on this process.

Patients who took 120 to 240 milligrams of ginkgo biloba extract for three to six months had a three percent increase in scores on memory tests, according to a study sponsored by the National Institute on Aging. These results, combined with those of three other recent tests, are being analyzed to determine if the herb offers a clear clinical benefit. Ginkgo biloba is a readily available natural product extracted from the leaves of the ginkgo biloba tree. It has been used as a Chinese herbal medicine for centuries and was recently approved in Germany to treat Alzheimer's.

Studies funded by the National Institute on Aging (NIA) have shown promising results for Vitamin E, the ingestion of which seems to slow Alzheimer's. Patients who took 2,000 I.U. of Vitamin E (alpha tocopoheral) daily were able to care for themselves and lived longer.

WATCH FOR HEALTH UPDATES

If you would like to keep abreast of the latest research being done on

TOP SECRET

AT LEAST WE KNOW THE OLD WAYS WORK

The older generation remembers how to use some of the old gadgets made before everything became electronic. However, many Y2K-conscious people are "going classic." Sales are up for wood-burning stoves, lanterns, food canners and juicers, and other non-electric "survivalist" gear. There are now more than 30,000 individually owned power-generating windmills in operation in this country, and the number is growing.

aging, you can visit the following Web sites:

- www.aoa.dhhs.gov/ elderpage. The Administration on Aging's site.

- www.cdc.gov/nccdphp. The Centers for Disease Control site.

- www.alzheimers.org/ index.html. The home of ADEAR, Alzheimer's Disease Education and Referral Center, a service of the NIA.

- www.nih.gov/nia. The official page for the NIA through the National Institute of Health.

You can also write for free pamphlets, newsletters, and factsheets. When requesting information in a letter, also ask to be placed on their mailing list.

- National Center for Injury Prevention and Control, Division of Unintentional Injury Prevention, Mailstop K60, 4770 Buford Highway NE, Atlanta, GA 30341-3724.

- Public Information Office, National Institute on Aging, Building 31, Room 5C27, 31 Center Drive MSC 2292, Bethesda, MD 20892-2292.

- The National Institute on Aging Information Center, P.O. Box 8057, Gaithersburg, MD 20898-8057; 800-222-2225, 800-222-4225 (Teletype compatible for the hard-of-hearing, or TTY).

GOVERNMENT AUCTION STEALS
What You Can Buy and How to Do It

★ ★ ★ ★

WHILE IT ISN'T THE BARGAIN-BIN spree that some unscrupulous marketers have made it out to be, a government surplus auction is a good way to get quality stuff at good prices. Buying used stuff from Uncle Sam is a great way to save. Remember, though, that you can find out about these auctions yourself. Don't pay a huge sum for auction information; it's all available for free. The government *wants* to sell its excess stuff. They will be happy to give you all the information you need.

BUYING IRS-SEIZED PROPERTY

Believe it or not, Uncle Sam does not enjoy taking property. He would much rather have the taxes that were owed on it. It's a big hassle to confiscate, store, and manage all this stuff. So help your country and yourself—buy real estate and other valuables taken from individuals and companies for nonpayment of taxes. Besides homes, buildings, and land lots, you can buy fine jewelry, all kinds of office equipment and supplies, televisions, VCRs, quality home furnishings, and other items.

Call the IRS number in your area (or in the area to which you are willing to travel) to get auction dates,

The Truth About Government Sales

1. Government property, land or otherwise, usually sells for close to market value. There are bargains, but you're not going to buy the rumored "House for a Dollar" or "Yacht for $100."

2. You need to be vigilant in checking out what is available and when.

3. You will face competition in the bidding.

catalogs, and lots of free information on how to buy stuff from the federal government. Remember, these agencies want to sell this surplus, so they will give you all the info you need.

Buying From U.S. Customs Office Seizures

This is property confiscated from smugglers. The goods are not illegal, but whoever tried to bring them into the country broke some laws in the process. It's true that a small portion of things prohibited in this country are sold on an "export only" basis. U.S. Customs-approved arrangements for shipping have to be made at the time of sale. These items are clearly labeled as such so that you cannot buy them by mistake.

You can find almost anything at these sales. Just think of all the items in an import store plus more: fine art, jewelry, wines, nonperishable foods, leather goods, china, and clothing.

Sale participants are required to register prior to each sale. Registration is free. Just bring a photo ID and receive your bidder number and a catalog, which contains a listing of merchandise to be sold and important information about the terms of sale. Phone bidding is even available on certain sales. Refer to flyers or recorded messages.

Beware of impostors. All advertisements for the Customs auctions will display the U.S. Customs Service seal and the EG&G Services name. This company is the sole contractor for the U.S. Customs Office.

For a fee, you can subscribe to a program and receive information two to three weeks before sale dates. The flyers include locations, dates, viewing and registration times, and a list of the property and merchandise for sale. Write or call for information: EG&G Services, Attention: CUS NET, 3702 Pender Drive, Suite 400, Fairfax, VA 22030-6066; 703-273-7373.

BUYING FROM THE ARMY CORPS OF ENGINEERS

The U.S. Army Corps of Engineers acquires single-family homes and other properties with up to two living units under the authority of a Homeowners Assistance Program (HAP). The HAP is for eligible applicants who cannot sell their homes under reasonable terms and conditions, as a result of a base closure or realignment action.

The properties are then offered for sale to the public. Local real estate brokers who sign a participation agreement with the HAP, and the agents who work for the broker, may show the properties to prospective buyers and submit offers on behalf of the buyer. In addition, local real estate agents will have information such as location of schools, churches, public transportation, and shopping centers.

LOOKING FOR A USED SUBMARINE?

Try the Defense Reutilization and Marketing Service Sales (DRMS), which offers some pretty unusual things—everything you can think of from the military. You can buy typewriters, computers, vehicles, aircraft components, engine accessories, office furniture and equipment, clothing, appliances, household paints and thinners, scrap iron, aluminum, copper, and paper. You can buy small boats and noncombatant ships, railroad cars, locomotives, and even *aircraft*. Business people are interested in these kinds of items, but lots of individuals convert the vehicles for civilian or commercial use, or use the parts on their own autos and trucks.

Get mailing list information through the DRMS by calling 888-352-9333. E-mail custservice@drms.dla.mil, or write: Defense Reutilization and Marketing Service, National Sales Office, 74 Washington Ave. N., Ste. 6, Battle Creek, MI 49017-3092.

BUYING FROM THE FEDERAL DEPOSIT INSURANCE CORPORATION

FDIC auctions offer the assets of failed bank loans. You can buy real estate, land, hotels, homes, shopping malls, and personal property—everything from computers, furniture, and phones to fine china, crystal, and antiques. Sales announcements will appear on the Internet, under "National Asset Sales Calendar—Real Estate Sales." They will also be advertised in local and regional newspapers.

BUYING AT GENERAL SERVICES ADMINISTRATION AUCTIONS

Stories about $100 yachts are pure fiction. If you're interested in buying used federal property, the government expects to receive a fair price. In fact, unless you're willing to pay close to market value, it is unlikely that you will be successful in purchasing *any* government surplus. Government vehicles have been purchased with your tax dollars, and to protect that investment, prices are set and items are seldom sold for less.

Most government vehicles were purchased new and

driven by government employees for official purposes. They are sold when they reach replacement age and/or mileage limitations. Used government vehicles are one of the best buys in the marketplace today; they are maintained well, have relatively low age and mileage, and have desired features like automatic transmission, air conditioning, power steering, and power brakes. They also come in attractive styles and colors.

Although you are not permitted to test drive GSA vehicles prior to sale, you may inspect sale property before making an offer (in fact, you are urged to do so). GSA personnel point out deficiencies when known, but take no responsibility for undisclosed problems. The "Condition of Property is not Warranted." Bid what the item is worth to *you*.

Remember to *look carefully*. When you see you can buy an army camouflage shirt

CONTACT NUMBERS FOR GSA AUCTIONS AND SALES

Great Lakes Region, Chicago, IL. www.gsa.gov/regions/r5/default.htm

Greater Southwest Region, Ft. Worth, TX. www.gsa.gov/regions/7fss/7fp/readme.htm

Heartland Region, Kansas City, MO. www.r6.gsa.gov/fss/auction.htm

New England Region, Boston, MA. Information: 617-565-1326

Northeast & Caribbean Region, New York, NY. Information: 212-264-4823

Northwest Region, Auburn, WA. www.northwest.gsa.gov/fss/prop_sup/persprop/schedule.htm

Pacific Rim Region, San Francisco, CA. Information: 415-522-2891

Rocky Mountain Region, Denver, CO. www.gsa.gov/regions/r8/fss/propmgt.htm

Southeast Sunbelt Region, Atlanta, GA. www.gsa.gov/regions/4k/fsssale.htm

for one dollar, it probably means that you can buy 200 of them for $200—a very different thing indeed. If you want a lifetime supply of quality shirts in mixed sizes, great. If you want to resell them at flea markets, great. These details aren't explained in the advertisements, however, and you could be disappointed after you send in your cash.

Plenty of government agencies want to dump excess goods, so keep your eyes open and look for those sales.

To get on a mailing list, you need to fill out a GSA Form 2170—Surplus Personal Property Mailing List Application. The form is available online at www.fss.gsa.gov. There is no application fee.

The GSA does not maintain a mailing list for vehicle auctions. If you wish to find out about upcoming sales, contact their hotline at 215-656-3400. This information is updated around the beginning of the month.

The GSA sells personal property by 1) sealed bid sales, 2) auctions, 3) fixed price sales, and 4) negotiated sales.

A sealed bid sale is for single items or items in isolated locations. An "Invitation for Bid" (IFB) is used by prospective buyers on mailing lists to submit an offer. The IFB contains item descriptions, sale terms and conditions, item locations and inspection times, and a bid form. Bid offers are submitted in a sealed envelope and mailed to a designated custodial office. Late bids are not accepted under any circumstance. Successful bidders are notified by mail.

Auctions are the most popular way for the public to buy government surplus property. The auctioneer "cries" the sale, orally soliciting bids, and "knocks down" each item to the highest responsive bidder. Auctions are a good way

WE HAVE MET THE ENEMY, AND HE IS US

The Information Security Department of the Project on Government Oversight (POGO) places the annual cost of the government's security classification system at about $5.6 billion. This estimate only includes the cost of physically safeguarding "secret" government information and doing background checks on people who apply for security clearance. The full cost could be as much as ten times higher.

property. Price tags are affixed to a variety of items, the majority being office furniture and computer equipment. Computer lovers will want to visit this site the last Friday of every month for an exclusive sale of computer equipment. Although property is sold via fixed price on a first-come, first-served basis, a steady stream of available federal surplus guarantees that attractive, desirable property is always just around the corner.

to buy cars, vans, trucks, plumbing and heating equipment, paper products, typewriters, computers and other office machines, or expensive items such as an airplane or large boat.

A fixed price sale is the federal government's way of providing the public with a familiar, easy-to-use method for purchasing

Negotiated sales are used for items of unusual interest such as X-ray equipment, mainframe computers, and items that require expedited disposal because of office closures or space constraints. The government faxes these customers who have expressed an interest in these sales or customers who have bid on these types of items in the past. These bids are generally faxed back within a week and awarded that same day. Payment is due within 48 hours of the award and is removed the next week.

Buying at HUD Auctions

HUD's single-family property sales are conducted by six management and marketing contractors. HUD is in the process of transferring files to these contractors who will soon begin to advertise properties for sale. Therefore, the sales program is temporarily suspended but will resume presently.

Each management and marketing contractor will list the properties on its own Web site. HUD will include a link to the contractor's Web site as soon as the single-family properties are available for purchase.

Buying From the U.S. Postal Service

Auctions of damaged or unclaimed items are held periodically at Mail Recovery Centers. To find out when auctions will be held, watch for ads in the newspaper or on televison. The post office has a real hodgepodge of offerings; apparently, people will mail anything.

Buying at SBA Auctions

The property in these databases was acquired by the

What To Do if You Suspect Fraud or False Advertising

If you suspect that you have been tricked or misled and/or you paid money for products or services that have little or no value, contact The U.S. Postal Service, the Federal Trade Commission, your state Attorneys General, your state and local consumer offices, and your local Better Business Bureau. All these offices are listed in the business or government listings of your local telephone directory.

U.S. Small Business Administration when administering its loan program and is available for purchase. The property ranges from real estate—commercial property, single-family homes, vacant land, and farms—to personal property such as machinery, equipment, furniture, fixtures, and inventory from a wide variety of business operations. For the sake of space, the database information on these properties is limited. You may call or visit the nearest SBA office in your location (your local phone book's government listings section has this information).

BUYING AT DEPARTMENT OF AGRICULTURE SALES

Here you may buy trucks, ambulances, station wagons, sedans, office equipment, office furniture, computers, and laboratory items from foreclosed farms. Check with your Rural Development (RD) county offices for dates and details of auctions and sales.

BUYING FROM THE DEPARTMENT OF ENERGY

The DOE sells office equipment, vehicles, furniture, trailers, generators, instruments, laboratory equipment, and mechanical power and transmission equipment. Sales are advertised in federal government buildings, national and local newspapers, and through radio and television announcements. You can also check the DOE Property Management Information Web site at www.pr.doe.gov/prprop.html for sales information.

BUYING FROM NASA

Want to buy a used space shuttle? Not for sale. But every year, $250 to $350 million in NASA surplus and personal property is sold to the public. They have computers, printers, electronics, testing equipment, office and laboratory equipment, video equipment, office paper, and recyclables like wire and metal cans.

Most of the sales follow a fairly regular schedule (accepting sealed bids or holding auctions) and take place directly at the 13 NASA locations. Advertisements are placed in local newspapers. NASA does not keep a buyer's mailing list, but you can check the Web site for announcements. Go to the NASA Sales page at www.hq.nasa.gov/office/codej/codejlg/nasasale.htm.

BUYING FROM THE GOVERNMENT PRINTING OFFICE

The GPO sells used printing and binding equipment as well as office furniture and business machines such as copiers, calculators, and typewriters. They are sold through sealed bids. Sales are advertised through bidder's lists and in the Commerce Business Daily. You can also fax a request for information to 202-512-1354.

BUYING FROM THE BUREAU OF LAND MANAGEMENT

This is as close to homesteading as you can get in the 20th century. Most of the land is actually part of the original public domain established during the western expansion in the early history of the United States. This is undeveloped land with no improvements. These tracts can be desert or rural; some parcels are a few acres, others are hundreds. They are usually scattered, isolated, or difficult to manage with little or no agricultural value. If you are looking for remote private living conditions that offer a real challenge, contact your local BLM office for information about sales. Be sure to examine the property to determine accessability, restrictions, and other conditions before making any bids.

TIPS ON BUYING FROM GOVERNMENT AUCTIONS

It is strongly recommended that you attend auction

previews. The preview is your only chance to get answers to your questions regarding merchandise, since items are sold as is and all sales are final. Merchandise is often not available for inspection on the day of sale.

Generally, a deposit is due the day of the sale and payment in full is due the following day. Purchases of $5,000 or less are usually required to be paid in full on the sale day. Payment is accepted by cash, cashier's check, or on some popular credit cards. Because cashiers cannot make change for more than ten percent of a cashier's check, it is recommended that you bring several cashier's checks in small denominations.

TOP SECRET

ONE OF THE GOOD GUYS

Brad Smith, the key person behind the U.S. State Department's international-rewards program, continually searched for tips and informants. When his health declined and his breathing grew labored, he used a respirator. When he lost command of his arms, he used a mouthpiece to work his computer. When Smith died, he was surfing the Internet for information on terrorist Osama bin Laden.

If you have difficulty locating the local offices of a particular sales program, call the Federal Information Center (FIC) for assistance. This service, provided by the U.S. GSA, can find the location of the sales office closest to you. Call toll-free, 800-688-9889 or 800-326-2996 (Telecommunications Device for the Deaf, TDD, or TTY).

THE MEDICARE MAZE

With a Little Knowledge, You Can Get Through It

★ ★ ★ ★

MOST PEOPLE KNOW that when they retire, they receive certain benefits—such as a monthly Social Security check. One of the benefits that comes with Social Security is Medicare, the government's version of health insurance. While at first there seems to be no rhyme or reason to what Medicare covers, don't worry; you don't have to be a rocket scientist to figure it out. Take your first step into the maze and read on.

WHO IS ELIGIBLE?

Medicare is a benefit of Social Security, and Social Security must be in place before Medicare can start. Even though you can begin drawing Social Security payments at age 62, Medicare does not begin until age 65. You qualify for Medicare based on your work record—ten years of work in which you have paid into FICA, the tax that bankrolls Medicare. If you don't think you've put in enough years at work, you may qualify based on your relationship to someone else who is qualified. Others who qualify:

- Widows and widowers, 65 or older, married to the deceased, Medicare-covered spouse at least one year before death.

- Divorced women and men, 65 or older, married for at least ten years to someone who is covered.

- Surviving parents, 65 or older, of a child receiving Social Security benefits who were receiving at least half of their support from that child's payments at the time of his or her death.

- Some legal immigrants, if they have lived in the U.S. five consecutive years and have Social Security eligibility.

- People with disabilities that prevent them from working.

If you have a question about *your* eligibility, call your local Social Security office.

MEDICARE FOR SALE

If you are age 65 and not eligible for Medicare, there is another option: You may choose to purchase it. Those who are not close to their work eligibility requirements will pay the highest price, but those who are close (about 2½ years from qualifying) may purchase it at a reduced cost.

GETTING THE MEDICARE BALL ROLLING

Just because you reach the magic age of 65 doesn't mean Medicare will magically appear in your benefits package. If you are already receiving Social Security checks, your enrollment will be automatic; otherwise, contact your local Social Security office about three months before your 65th birthday to find out what to do.

THE HOSPITAL FACTS

Medicare Part A deals with hospital costs. It does not pay for or cover everything, but on the bright side, there is no cost for Part A (which has been financed by FICA).

Part A covers service in hospitals, skilled nursing facilities, and home health and hospice care. The exact dollar amount of coverage varies from year to year. To learn what coverage you can expect, call your local Social Security office and request a copy of "Medicare and You," or download it from the Medicare Web site at www.medicare.gov.

Coverage includes:
- A semiprivate room
- Meals
- Nursing and medical service and supplies

Coverage does not include:
- A private duty nurse
- A private room, unless in the case of medical necessity
- Television
- Telephone

DON'T GET CAUGHT IN THE TRAP

It's a common misconception that Medicare pays for long-term or permanent nursing home care. *It does not.* Custodial and personal care services are not covered at all. The only coverage is for rehabilitation, and even then reimbursed care is limited to 100 days.

FREE CARE

Home health coverage is a provision of Part A. The good news is that except for the 20 percent copayment you must make on medical equipment, the actual home health service is free to you. Medicare picks up the entire tab.

A TRIP TO THE DOCTOR

Medicare Part B covers services such as seeing your doctor, lab tests, X rays, and other medical procedures done on an outpatient basis. It does not cover dental work, hearing aids, eyeglasses (except the first pair after cataract surgery), or prescription drugs, unless the drugs are administered in the hospital or a skilled nursing facility. Part B is optional, and it will cost you just under $50 per month with a $100 yearly deductible. The government pays part of the bill, and you pay the rest. Part B rates change yearly, so consult "Medicare and You" for current rates.

HOW DO I FILE A CLAIM?

The good news is that you don't. Claims are filed by your medical providers.

NOT EXACTLY SECRETS, BUT...

Even the Medicare experts have to check the book to find out everything there is to know. Two things *you* should know, without having to check the book, can make your journey into the maze a little easier.

- You are not required to pay for services Medicare has refused to pay *if you did not know* the service was not covered by Medicare, or if you did not have the expertise to know the service was not medically necessary.

- Even though Part B is optional, it is not available all the time. If you enroll at the time you enroll in part A, you will receive the lowest monthly payment. Enrollment after that can only be done during the open period between January 1 and March 31 of every year. Your premium will increase ten percent a year for every year you wait. So if you want it, get it at the beginning.

IS YOUR DOCTOR RIPPING OFF MEDICARE?

Find a copy of "Fraud and Abuse" on the Web site at www.medicare.gov, or call 800-MEDICARE for a copy. Learn how to spot fraud and how to claim a reward when you do. Medicare is clamping down on abuse, so you might as well profit from it if you can.

GET PART B FOR FREE

Some low-income Medicare beneficiaries are entitled to have their Part B premiums, deductibles, and copayments paid by their state's Medicaid agency. Medicaid is a federal program offered through the state that provides medical care for the poor. To see if you are eligible to become a Qualified Medicare Beneficiary (QMB), contact your nearest welfare office or call Social Security at 800-772-1213. If you do not qualify for that program, ask about qualifying as a Specified Low-Income Medicare Beneficiary (SLMB). Deductibles and copayments are not paid for, but part or all of the Part B premiums are.

TOP SECRET

DREAM DAYS FOR DIPLOMATS

High-ranking U.N. officials have diplomatic immunity from criminal action filed by U.S. courts, so the organization has become a haven for deadbeat dads. Their pay and pensions cannot be claimed by national courts.... Foreign diplomats in the U.S. cannot be arrested, do not have to pay taxes, pay parking or speeding tickets, honor contracts, pay debts, or face the consequences of breaking laws.

Why Pay More?

Assignment is probably the most important word to understand when you become a Medicare beneficiary. You'll hear it over and over, and unless you know what it is, you could wind up paying more money for your services.

Medicare assigns a dollar amount for each of its services, and it will pay no more for that service. Many medical providers agree to accept what Medicare assigns, and Medicare will usually cover about 80 percent of its assigned dollar value while you will pay 20 percent. Medical providers in all states (except Massachusetts, Rhode Island, and Pennsylvania) are not bound to accept the Medicare-assigned value, which means they can charge you more. If that happens, you are responsible to make up the difference between what Medicare will pay and what your doctor will charge. So always ask, "Do you accept assignment?" If your doctor does not, ask for a discount. Doctors do give them.

The Times They Are A-Changin'

Traditionally, Medicare has paid for illnesses as they happen, but a desire to prevent illness before it happens has brought about interesting changes. Some preventative procedures are now covered, such as:

- Mammogram, once a year.

- Pap smear and pelvic exam, including a clinical breast exam, once every three years. If you are at high risk for cervical or vaginal cancer, or have had an abnormal Pap smear in the preceding three years, these tests will be covered every year.

- Fecal occult blood test to detect colon cancer, once a year.

- Flexible sigmoidoscopy to

detect colon cancer once every four years.

- Colonoscopy once every two years if you are a high risk of colon cancer.

- Barium enema may be substituted for either the sigmoidoscopy or the colonoscopy.

- Diabetes monitoring, including glucose monitors, test strips, lancets, and self-management training.

- Bone mass measurement. The frequency varies with your health status.

- Flu shot, once a year.

- Pneumococcal vaccination. Your doctor will determine how often you need it.

- Hepatitis B vaccination, if you meet a risk criteria determined by your doctor.

EVEN MORE CHANGES

The traditional fee-for-services is one of several health insurances, some of which are offered by Medicare. A privately sold supplement called Medigap, that adds to your Medicare coverage, has been available for quite some time. It comes in ten standardized policies available for purchase from private insurance companies in your area. To learn more about Medigap insurance, pick up a copy of "Guide to Health Insurance for People With Medicare" from your local Medicare or Social Security office, or get it online at www.medicare.gov under the section marked "Publications." Call your state insurance commissioner for a list of companies offering Medigap.

Other Medicare Options:

- Managed Care pays medical providers a fixed amount of money to treat Medicare beneficiaries. You will not need to add a supplemental policy to your care. There is no need to worry about cost before seeking treatment because this is not a fee-for-service plan.

TIPS FOR GETTING THROUGH THE MAZE

Even armed with knowledge, it isn't easy. Medicare is not often user-friendly. These five simple tips can help you move through the maze and get the services you need. Taking the initiative puts you in charge of your medical care, and knowing the answers will help you plow through the Medicare maze.

1. Find a doctor who is a Medicare physician.

2. Ask for a fee schedule for office visits, procedures, and testing.

3. Ask if medical bills are itemized.

4. Ask if the test or procedure your doctor is about to prescribe is medically necessary and why.

5. Ask if the test or procedure is covered by Medicare. If it is not, ask if an alternative procedure *is* covered by Medicare.

- Private fee-for-service policies allow you to buy medical insurance from a private insurance agency. Medicare pays your premium each month, then pays no more. Neither you nor your physician can make claims to Medicare under this plan.

Finally, Medicare Medical Savings Account Plan, a test program, allows you to buy health insurance from a private company approved by Medicare, then opens a Medicare Savings Account (MSA) at a bank or other financial institution also approved by Medicare.

At the beginning of the year, Medicare will deposit money into your account for paying medical bills and will also pay the monthly premium to the insurance company. You must continue to pay your monthly Part B premium. When you need medical money for expenses not covered by your insurance policy or Part B, you withdraw it from your account. When the account is empty, the rest comes out of your pocket. You must keep the account for a full year, and enrollment takes place every November. Money can accumulate from year to year; if you don't spend it, you can use that leftover money for things other than medical care—but you *will* be taxed on it. Money used for medical purposes is *not* taxed.

For more details on any of Medicare's choices, visit the Medicare Web site (www.medicare.gov) and download copies of "Understanding Your Medicare Choices" and "Worksheet for Comparing Medicare Health Plans." You can also get them from your local Social Security office. More information is available by calling the Medicare Special Information number at 800-633-4227.

TOP SECRET

THE HIGH COST OF CONGRESS

Members of Congress get free personal printing privileges. One Florida congressional leader had more than 400 items printed that cost taxpayers $405,000....In 1995, U.S. Representative Frederick K. Heineman (R–NC) said that his combined congressional salary and pension ($183,000 annually) made him "lower-middle class." He noted that an income of $300,000 to $750,000 a year is actually "middle class."

AND FINALLY....

If you don't like Medicare's decision, appeal it. You will receive a summary statement of services, called a Medical Summary Notice (MSN). Instructions for appealing are on the back. Most people don't contest bad decisions, and that saves Medicare money. Don't let a bad decision cost you. Appeal it!

PLANNING A TRIP?

Guess Who Has the Information to Make That Trip Easier?

★ ★ ★ ★

IF YOU'VE READ THIS FAR, you've probably guessed that Uncle Sam has a treasure trove of travel information just for the asking. When he's in an especially generous mood, there are even a few trips you can take on *his* tab. Don't pack your bags yet, but keep them handy just in case.

CUBAN CIGARS, CDS, AND YOUR CUSTOMS DECLARATION

Don't get stuck hauling that 3,000-pound, 300-year-old turtle from the Galapagos Islands halfway around the world only to find that you can't bring it in once you reach the States. U.S. Customs has strict rules about what can cross their borders, either coming or going, and those rules also pertain to trademark items, such as computer software, books, and videotapes. Prescription medications have their own set of rules, too, as do sausages and certain items with feathers. In order to learn what can and can't travel with you, visit the U.S. Customs Web site at www.customs.ustreas.gov. You can also write to: Department of the Treasury, U.S. Customs Service, P.O. Box 7407, Washington, DC 20229.

You may also call 202-927-6724 to request a copy of

Know Before You Go, a brochure detailing almost everything you will need to know about what U.S. Customs expects when you travel. The document can also be downloaded from the U.S. Customs Web site.

CLAIM SOME CASH FROM CUSTOMS

U.S. Customs doesn't take smuggling lightly. To prove it, they've set up a reward system for good citizens who report drug smuggling. You remain anonymous at all times, and if the report leads to a conviction, you could receive a cash reward. For more information, or to report a suspected incident involving drug smuggling into the United States, call 800-BE-ALERT.

DON'T PACK A PEST

U.S. Customs isn't the only branch of the government concerned with what you're bringing back into the country. The United States Department of Agriculture also keeps watch by way of its Animal and Plant Health Inspection Service (APHIS). They're on the lookout for that one piece of fruit with fruit flies or that contaminated sausage carrying the virus responsible for foot-and-mouth disease. It only takes one small contaminant to cause an outbreak, so they're pretty picky about their search. If they find that banana you didn't declare, it could cost you big bucks in fines. Find out what APHIS expects at www.aphis.usda.gov, or request a list of what APHIS does and doesn't allow from: APHIS, 4700 River Road, Riverdale, MD 20737.

JUST IN CASE YOU HAVEN'T BEEN WARNED ENOUGH

The Department of State has its own warnings for travelers, too. You can learn everything you need to know about passports, including how to locate a passport agency near your home. You'll also pick up tips on preparing for your trip, health precautions,

U.S. embassies and consulates, and how to handle your money (including using those omnipresent ATMs that are now available abroad).

The Web site is travel.state.gov (no "www"). For passport information, you can also call the National Passport Information Center at 900-225-5674.

Call the Office of American Citizens Services at 202-647-5225 for information on travel safety while you're at it.

BEFORE YOU CROSS THE BORDER

If you're headed to Angola, do you know what disease outbreaks in that country might affect you? Have you had the right immunizations for a trip to the Sudan? Do you know what to do to prevent typhoid, travelers' diarrhea, malaria, yellow fever, or hepatitis A or B?

Don't take that trip without first contacting the Centers for Disease Control and Prevention (CDC) to find out everything you need to know about potential health risks and what to do about them. Visit the

TOP SECRET

BUDGET CONSCIOUS?

In October 1995, the federal government reopened a large office building in Binghamton, NY, more than 13 years after it had been closed due to a small electrical fire that spread deadly chemicals around the building. The government spent more than $53 million in cleaning, gutting, and restoring the inside, then cleaning it again to pass federal inspection. The building had only cost $17 million to build in the first place.

Travelers' Health section of the CDC web site at www.cdc.gov or request a packet of travel information from: Centers for Disease Control and Prevention, 1600 Clifton Road NE, Atlanta, GA 30300.

You may also call 800-311-3435 with the request. For a current update on travel alerts, call 888-232-3228.

GIVE ME LAND, LOTS OF LAND

It'll be under those starry skies above, and you won't be fenced in. The USDA Forest Service, along with the U.S. Army Corps of Engineers, offers more than 49,000 camping facilities at 1,700 different locations throughout the United States. Whether you're looking for a wilderness experience, the day use of a shelter, a flat spot on which to pitch a tent, or a cabin in the woods for you and a loved one (or you and ten of your best friends), federal lands are waiting for you to find and reserve them.

The National Recreation Reservation Service at 877-444-6777 handles the reservations, but you must know where the sites are before you call. Find *that* info at www.reserveusa.com.

LEAVE NO TRACE

Are you in the mood to teach responsible outdoor recreation, do-no-damage camping skills, wildlife ethics, protection of wilderness resources, and other backcountry skills? Leave No Trace, jointly authorized by the National Park Service, U.S. Fish and Wildlife Service, U.S. Forest Service, and Bureau of Land Management, will teach you the skills to take care of the wilderness and then show you how to teach those skills to others. The training costs approximately $650, but scholarships are available.

For more information, contact: Leave No Trace, P.O. Box 997, Boulder, CO 80306, call 800-332-4100, or check the Web site at www.lnt.org.

On this site, you'll see detailed information about each of the camping areas, including fees, accessibility, and the kind of trees under which you'll be taking your afternoon nap. You'll also find information about when your perfect campsite or cabin is available for rent. You can make your reservation online, too.

MORE FUN ON FEDERAL LANDS COURTESY OF THE NET

Visit the Web sites at www.recreation.gov, www.fs.fed.us, or www.blm.gov to see which of Uncle Sam's other great outdoor adventures await you. Tap into a source for U.S. Geological Survey maps, find a few wild and scenic rivers, and learn about the wilderness tools you'll need if you choose to get back to nature for a week or two. Also, pick up weather forecasts, accessibility information, and information on fees and special-use permits.

The easiest way to get everything you need to determine the location and type of vacation you want on federal land is to go online, but you may also request a packet of information on recreational services from: USDA Forest Service, PO Box 96090, Washington, DC 20090-6090.

THIS TRIP'S ON UNCLE SAM

But you've got to work to get it. As a Peace Corps volunteer, you will have the opportunity to travel to new places and meet new people. You'll get to live abroad, learn new languages, and become part of another culture. All you have to do is a little work in turn for the rewarding experiences you'll receive. You might teach math or English, help protect the area's environment, get involved in health and nutrition projects, or teach people how to plant a crop—in other words, you will help improve the world at the grass-roots level. (The oldest Peace Corps volunteer, by the way, was 86 years young.)

If you've got a year or so to give, call the Peace Corps at 800-424-8580 or check the Web site at www. peacecorps.gov.

SPEAKING OF TRIPS

The mission of the United States Information Agency (USIA) is to understand, inform and influence foreign policy by promoting national interests abroad. You probably never thought that could involve *you*. Well, it can if you have a background in any of the areas in which the USIA is currently recruiting speakers and workshop leaders. The government will cover your expenses.

About 850 people are chosen to represent the United States every year. They come from different backgrounds—government, academia, the media, and business—and their topics range from nuclear proliferation to how to succeed in running a small business.

For more information, visit the Web site at www. usia.gov or call Office of Thematic Programs at 202-619-4210.

NEED A LITTLE SAX?

Well, Uncle Sam does, and he sends a small number of American jazz duos to countries that lack exposure to American cultural achievement. Maybe you're an artist in need of a little cultural exchange in a foreign country. If so, find information on the USIA Web site at www.usia.gov, or call 202-619-4779.

FACE TO FACE WITH THE FEDS

Want to meet this Uncle Sam face to face? It's not as difficult as you think. If you can get to Washington, DC, you can take a free tour of the Capitol and the White House.

Guided tours of the Capitol are available daily. If you

don't want to go with the group, you can pick up a brochure and guide yourself through the building in which elected officials are hard at work. And, yes, if you pass a congressional representative in the hallway, you *can* put in your two cents worth. For updated information on visiting the Capitol, call 202-225-6827. Information is also available online at www.house.gov.

Do You Peek in Other Peoples' Closets?

When you get to the White House, you probably won't see the President (or his closet), but a free White House tour *will* take you past the library and the state dining rooms, and you'll get to peek in the east, green, blue, and red rooms as well.

In peak seasons (from the third Tuesday in March until the Saturday before Labor Day and through the entire month of December), you'll need free tickets for the tour. They can be picked up at the Visitor Center on the corner of 15th and E Streets, and they are not available in advance. The doors open at

---

TOP SECRET

WHAT'S *YOUR* WORST ARMY STORY?

A December 1995 report in the *Air Force Times* stated that soldier Joseph Cannon, who had recently finished a six-year term in the Army, was never paid after boot camp. He had missed 144 paychecks totaling more than $103,000, but never complained. Cannon, whose records were lost by the paymaster on his initial assignment, lived in the barracks and ate only in the mess hall.

DID GEORGE WASHINGTON REALLY SLEEP HERE?

The National Trust for Historic Preservation, chartered by Congress in 1949, has a list of historic hotels that might have lodged that famous man a night or two. Online at www.nthp.org, you will find a state-by-state directory of historic hotels plus information on historic driving tours. If you're looking for that special bed where he really did sleep, check it out.

7:30 A.M., so you'd better get there early.

General tour information is available by calling 202-456-7041 (TTY 202-456-2121), or online at www.whitehouse.gov.

WHO SAYS UNCLE SAM DOESN'T RECOGNIZE YOU PERSONALLY?

He can, in the form of a White House tour personally guided by a congressional representative or senator. Contact the Washington office of your congressional representative at least ten weeks in advance of your trip and request tickets for a Congressional Guided Tour.

You can find the office for your congressional representatives online at www.house.gov or www.senate.gov, or call 202-224-3121.

PASSPORT IN TIME

Would you like to work with an archaeologist or a historian, or in a national forest or grassland? These opportunities, and many more, are available to you when you become a Passport in Time (PIT) volunteer for the USDA Forest Service. You literally get to take a trip in search of American history, and your incidental expenses (including transportation, uniforms, lodging, and food) will be paid. For more information, contact: Passport In Time Clearinghouse, P.O. Box 31315, Tucson, AZ 85751-1315, or call 800-281-9176 (voice or TTY).

ATTEN—TION!

The VA Offers Benefits Worthy of a Salute

★ ★ ★ ★

DID YOU KNOW that eligible veterans can receive trips or a yearly clothing allowance? Most people know that the Veterans Administration offers benefits to military veterans, but they don't have a clue about what exactly is available. For instance, you may not know that members of 29 different nonmilitary organizations are *also* eligible for VA benefits. Read on to see if some lesser-known benefits could help you or your family.

LOST A SERVICE MEDAL, DECORATION, OR AWARD?

It may take up to two years, but your branch of the military will replace it for free. Call 800-827-1000 to request a Standard Form (SF180) Request Pertaining to Military Records. Send it to 9700 Page Ave., St. Louis, MO 63132-5100. Address it to the appropriate service branch:

- Army: National Personnel Records Center, Medals Section

- Air Force, Army Air Corps & Army Air Forces: National Personnel Records Center, Air Force Reference

- Navy, Marine & Coast Guard: Bureau of Naval Personnel Liaison Office, Room 5409

LOOKING FOR AN OLD MILITARY BUDDY?

Write a message to your buddy and stick it in an unsealed, stamped envelope. Include a note to the VA explaining who you are trying to reach and offer as much information as you can to identify your old servicemate. Then, put everything in a large envelope and send it to your nearest VA regional office. (Find the address in the government section of your phone book.) Due to privacy restrictions, the VA will not give you information about the friend you are trying to find, but it will forward your message if your friend is still listed in the VA files.

BENEFITS THAT COULD BE YOURS

The range of VA disability benefits, especially for service-connected disabilities, spans from vocational rehabilitation to education to medical services. Here are a few not-so-common benefits for eligible veterans with disabilities.

- $38,000 for building, buying or adapting a home.

- $5,500 auto assistance for adaptive auto equipment.

- Yearly clothing allowances for veterans with prosthetic or orthopedic appliances or who have a skin condition that requires a medication that can ruin clothing.

Contact your regional VA office to see whether you qualify for such benefits.

GET HELP BUYING YOUR HOME

Most people think the VA is a lending institution for home loans, but it is actually a guarantor of loans originating with a conventional lending institution. The VA will guarantee only part of the total loan, but that guarantee makes the loan easier to secure and in some cases helps lower the interest rate. An exception to the loan policy is made for Native American veterans who are eligible to receive a direct VA loan for buying a home on Native American trust land.

Others, besides veterans, eligible for the loan guarantee include:

- An unremarried surviving spouse of a service member who died on active duty or of a service-connected cause.

- A spouse of an active-duty military member either missing in action or being held as a prisoner of war for at least 90 days.

- A U.S. citizen who served in the armed forces of a U.S. ally during World War II.

- A member of an organization with recognized military-related contributions to the World War II effort of the United States. Members of those organizations are eligible for other benefits, too.

For a list of the organizations, or to learn more about the VA loan guarantee or the Native American Direct Home Loan, call 800-827-1000.

SPINA BIFIDA

Children with spina bifida who are dependents of Vietnam veterans are now

SHOW ME THE MONEY

Today, there are around 25.6 million veterans, and a total of about 70 million people—veterans, dependents, and survivors of deceased veterans—who may be eligible for benefits. Those benefits total nearly $44 billion a year, with more than $23 billion paid out in benefit programs and $18 billion for medical programs. Fifty-four percent of all VA expenditures go for direct payments such as compensation, pensions, and educational benefits. Forty-two percent is spent on medical care, and less than one percent goes to construction programs in hospitals, national cemeteries, and other VA facilities. A little more than two percent is spent on general operating expenses.

eligible for VA medical care, vocational training, and a monthly allowance. More information is available at your local VA health care facility.

A FEW BURIAL FACTS

The VA offers burial benefits for all veterans discharged other than dishonorably. Benefits for those in a national or state-owned cemetery for veterans include a grave site, a memorial plot for those whose remains were not available, a headstone, a flag to drape the casket, and some burial expense reimbursement.

- Information inscribed on headstones is standard: name, branch of service, and birth and death years. If requested by the cemetery, other information can be included, such as military rank, war in which the veteran served, religious emblem, and any awards won.

- If burial is outside a national cemetery, the VA will supply a headstone, but will not pay to place it on the grave. To apply, call 800-697-6947, or send form VA 40-1330, available from VA regional offices, to: Director of Memorial Programs (403A), National Cemetery System, Department of Veterans Affairs, Washington, DC 20420.

- Headstones are provided for veterans with unmarked grave sites not in this country.

- Presidential Memorial Certificates, bearing the signature of the President of the United States, are given to next of kin or other loved ones of deceased honorably discharged veterans.

- To learn the burial location of a veteran thought to be buried in a national cemetery, write a letter with the request, including the veteran's full name, service branch, date and place of birth and death, and state from which the veteran entered into active duty. Send the information to: U.S. Department of Veterans Affairs, National Cemetery Administration (402B), Burial Location Request, 810 Vermont Ave. NW, Washington, DC 20420.

For a list of non-veterans eligible for burial benefits, plus other burial information, call 800-827-1000, or just visit this Web site: www.va. gov.

More Than Just a Trip to the Doctor

Benefits for VA health care and dental programs are available to veterans on a priority basis, with service-connected conditions topping the list. To determine your eligibility, and to request information on all health care benefits, call the VA health care facility nearest you. If you are a Gulf War veteran, information on specific Gulf benefits is available at 800-749-8387 (800-PGW-VETS).

Besides the normal health care options outlined in "Federal Benefits for Veterans and Dependents," available for $5 from the Consumer Information Center, Pueblo, CO 81009 (or downloaded free at www.pueblo.gsa.gov), the VA operates several programs to assist older or chronically ill veterans. To learn more about the following programs, contact your nearest VA health care facility.

- Hospice care is provided in both home and in-patient settings for persons in the last phases of an incurable disease. Bereavement counseling is also offered to the family following the death of a patient.

- Home Based Primary Care (HBPC) provides in-home care to severely disabled or chronically ill veterans.

- Domiciliary Care is a residential rehabilitation and health maintenance cen-

DON'T COUNT YOUR BILLS BEFORE THEY HATCH

The U.S. Treasury Department, confident that its technology was secure, spent $32 million on a worldwide public relations campaign to spread the word about the supposedly counterfeit-proof $100 bill. Unfortunately, events did not follow the PR plan. Within two months, the Secret Service found that more than a dozen counterfeits of the new bill had turned up in U.S. stores.

ter for veterans who do not require full-time medical care but who cannot live independently.

- The Alzheimer's/Dementia Program offers services for veterans with Alzheimer's disease or related dementias.

- The Adult Day Health Care program provides rehabilitation and maintenance services and helps participants and their caregivers develop the skills needed to manage care at home.

- Respite Care allows veterans to stay in a VA health care facility on a short-term basis, giving the regular caregiver a break from the burden of daily care.

JUST FOR WOMEN

Women make up 14 percent of the current active duty military force and about four percent of the total veteran population. By the year 2010, an estimated 10 percent of the veteran population will be women. Women veterans are entitled to the same benefits as male veterans, but the VA includes special services and programs designed to meet the health care needs of women.

- Breast exams, Pap smears, menopause advice, and sexual trauma counseling are available from all VA health care centers.

- The National Mammography HelpLine is 888-492-7844.

Want to Study in Europe?

The VA offers different options for education and vocational training to veterans, but educational assistance is available to the children and unremarried spouses of eligible deceased veterans in the form of financial aid for:

- College degrees, including independent study, cooperative training, and study-abroad programs.

- Certificates or diplomas from trade, business, or vocational schools.

- On-the-job training situations, including apprenticeships and farm cooperative courses.

Eligible children over 14 years of age with a physical or mental disability that impairs participation in an educational program may receive restorative training to overcome that disability. Training available includes:

- Speech and voice correction.

- Language retraining.

Who Are the Vets?

Some 2.7 million veterans receive disability compensations. More than 628,000 widows, children, and parents of deceased veterans currently get survivor compensation and death benefits. Survivors of the Vietnam era total an estimated 128,000, and more than 315,000 veterans from World War II survive. The last dependent of a Revolutionary War veteran died in 1911. The war of 1812's last dependent died in 1946, and the Mexican War's last survivor died in 1962. Slightly more than 900 children and widows of Spanish-American War veterans still receive VA compensation.

- Auditory training.

- Lip reading.

- Braille reading and writing.

- Vocational training for those who cannot complete an educational program.

For more information on veteran and dependent educational benefits, call the HelpLine at 888-442-4551 or visit the Web site at www.va.gov/education.

TAP YOUR WAY TO A FREE TRIP

Do you have a creative flair, perhaps for dancing, painting, or acting? Then brush off those tap shoes! If you currently participate in a recreational therapy program at your local VA facility, ask about a trip to the National Veterans Creative Arts Competition. Travel to and from this event is provided by your local VA facility, and the tab for housing, meals, ground transportation, and other expenses is covered by the National Committee.

Funds are also available for other events involving veterans undergoing rehabilitation care, so check with your VA therapist to see if you qualify for:

- The National Veterans Golden Age Games, a sports and recreational competition for veterans over 55.

- The National Disabled Veterans Winter Sports Clinic, which instructs severely disabled veterans in adaptive Alpine and Nordic skiing.

- The National Veterans Wheelchair Games, a multi-event sports and rehabilitation program.

OTHERS OFFER VA BENEFITS, TOO

Some benefits are not given by the VA but by agencies working with the Department of Veterans Affairs.

Check with your state employment office for the following:

- Job-Finding Assistance. Free counseling, testing, referral, and job placement are provided. Veterans are given top priority, with disabled vets receiving highest consideration.

- Job-Training Partnership. This is a job-training program for disabled Vietnam-era vets and veterans who have recently left military service.

- Disabled Veterans Outreach. This program locates disabled veterans and helps them find jobs.

- Unemployment Compensation. This may be paid to discharged service members for a limited time.

More non-VA benefits:

TOP SECRET

THE COST OF PREPAREDNESS

Multinational corporations are spending unimaginable sums to protect against Y2K computer malfunction. After originally budgeting $300 million for Y2K preparation, AT&T has come closer to spending $900 million. General Motors' figure is said to be nearly that high. Brokerage firm Merrill Lynch is said to be spending more than $550 million to ensure the accurate tracking of data in its customers' accounts.

- Veterans Readjustment Appointment (VRA), which promotes job opportunities for veterans within the federal government. Veterans seeking VRA should apply directly to the government agency at which they wish to work.

- The Federal Housing Administration Home Mortgage Insurance

Program for Veterans requires less down payment than other FHA programs. Submit form VA 26-8261a, available at any VA office, for a Certificate of Veteran Status. Give the certificate to your lender, who will submit it to the FHA.

- Naturalization preference is given to aliens with honorable service in the U.S. Armed Forces during hostilities. They may be naturalized without completing the general requirements for naturalization.

- The Small Business Administration provides training, counseling, and advice on surety bonding and financial management to veterans operating small businesses. It also guarantees small business loans under its Loan Guarantee Program. For more information, call the nearest SBA office at 800-827-5722.

- Passports can cost as much as $75, but they are free for family members visiting overseas graves of World War I and World War II dead. Contact the American Battle Monuments Commission, Courthouse Plaza II, Suite 500, 2300 Clarendon Blvd., Arlington, VA 22201.

- Unlimited commissary and exchange privileges at military installations based in the U.S. are available to honorably discharged veterans with a 100 percent service-related disability, unremarried surviving spouses, retired members of the U.S. Armed Forces, Medal of Honor recipients, and their dependents or orphans.

The VA offers literally hundreds of additional benefits to eligible veterans. To establish eligibility, or to learn more about anything you have read in this chapter, call 800-827-1000.

WHY PAY FULL PRICE WHEN YOU DON'T HAVE TO?

Uncle Sam Has a Few Discounts up His Sleeve

★ ★ ★ ★

NO ONE *LIKES* TO PAY full price for anything. So why *should* they? Discounts on almost every product and every service are available to the savvy negotiator. However, you don't have to be a slick talker to take advantage of the discounts offered by the government. All you have to do is meet certain eligibility requirements (one of which is being at least 62), to receive discounts on everything from moving to the country to parking your RV in a national park.

THREE LITTLE HOUSING DISCOUNTS FROM UNCLE SAM

You won't qualify if you intend to rent something comparable to the Taj Mahal, but government funding *is* available for older Americans having difficulty making house payments. Three programs, all managed by local housing authorities, provide money to reduce the cost of housing. There are waiting lists, but be patient; the money you save could be worth the wait.

- Public housing is typically in a HUD-approved (Department of Housing and Urban Development) complex. This program requires tenants to pay no more than 30 percent of their monthly income.

- Section 8 Rental Certificate recipients may live where they wish, subject to HUD approval, and are given vouchers that adjust monthly rent to 30 percent of their monthly income.

- Section 202 housing, the only one of HUD's housing programs specifically for seniors, supports seniors in housing where other services, such as transportation or meals, are made available. Again, the rent will not exceed 30 percent of the resident's adjusted monthly income.

Preference for housing subsidy usually goes to:

1. Those who pay housing costs, including utilities, in excess of 50 percent of their monthly income.

2. Those being involuntarily evicted, such as by fire or threat of violence.

3. Those who currently live in substandard housing.

For more information on any of the programs, check the Housing and Urban Development Web site at www.hud.gov and click on the section marked "Rental Help." You can also click the search function at the top of the page, then scan down to "Senior Citizens"—or call the HUD regional office listed in the blue pages of your local phone book.

A TEENY, TINY BIT OF HELP

For seniors living in HUD-subsidized houses in certain parts of the country, programs offer discounted living assistance to those in need. It may involve providing a hot meal every day, housekeeping, or assisting with personal care. The portion of the bill *you* pay for the service is substantially reduced. However, these programs are rare, and funding for them is not exactly flowing from Congress. So, if you are living in a HUD house (or you will be), check with your HUD regional offices, listed in the blue pages of your phone book, to see if a Congregate Housing Services Program is available in your area.

LIFE ON THE FARM IS KINDA' LAID BACK

If you're beginning to feel the squeeze of the city or you're tired of the noise and smog, think country. The Rural Housing Service, a branch of the United States Department of Agriculture, offers several incentives to get you to the country or to a small town. Low-cost home ownership loans, discounted rural rental housing loans, rental assistance, and discounted congregate housing for seniors are just a few of your country-living options. For more information, visit the web site at www.rurdev. usda.gov. You may also call the Office of USDA Rural Development at 202-720-4323 or write to: USDA Rural Development, Stop 0705, 1400 Independence Ave. SW, Washington, DC 20250-0705.

LET A BUDDY SHARE THE COST

One of the best rent or mortgage discounts available involves finding someone to share the cost. You may actually be able to reduce your house payments and utilities by half if you rent out that spare bedroom. If you don't have a place of your own to rent out, you could still save half on your living expenses by moving in with someone who does. So if you're willing to save money, but you don't have a buddy who can move in and you don't know anyone who will let *you* move in, what then?

Shared housing opportunities can be located through ElderCare Locator, a public service of the Administration on Aging and the U.S. Department of Health and Human Services. The search is free, so if you're stuck in a cold, dark climate and would

WHAT THAT MEDICARE CARD CAN DO

Senior citizen discounts are almost everywhere these days. Restaurants, movie theaters, and eyeglass companies offer them. They are available in department stores and grocery stores. Museum admission costs can be discounted. So can tickets to the opera or an NBA game or a visit to the zoo. Ten percent is the customary senior discount, but some places offer higher discounts on a designated "senior citizens day."

So what do you do if you're 70 and look 50 (other than be eternally grateful for your good fortune)? It's simple: Produce your Medicare card. Any establishment that offers the discount will accept Uncle Sam's word that you are the right age. But not only do you have to keep the card with you at all times, you also have to go one step further. *You have to ask for the discount.* Most of the time it will not be offered automatically, and often it will not even be advertised. But no matter where you go or what you do, be ready to grab your card and pop the question: "Do you offer a senior discount?"

prefer to find someone who needs a roommate in a warm, sunny place, that option is available, too. For more information on getting (or becoming) a roommate, call 800-677-1116.

SAY YOU DON'T GET AROUND MUCH ANYMORE?

A program funded under the Older Americans Act discounts local transportation for seniors. To find local transit providers who receive federal money to provide transportation to seniors, call the National Transit Hotline at 800-527-8279. You may also call ElderCare Locator at 800-677-1116 for information on discounted transportation in your area.

GOVERNMENT HELP TO MODIFY YOUR HOME

Maybe you need something as simple as grab bars in your shower. Maybe it's something a little more complicated, such as a ramp to your front door. Whatever the modification or repair, funds are allocated under the Older American's Act to help reduce the cost of what you need. For more information, call

TOP SECRET

THIS WINDFALL IS BARELY A BREEZE

The good news is that in 1998, the U.S. Department of Justice received a check for $5.6 million. The late Stanley S. Newburg, a private citizen, ordered that his estate be left to the government as thanks for having been let into the country as an émigré from Austria in 1906. The bad news is that based on the 1998 federal budget, Mr. Newburg's gift covers about two minutes' worth of government spending.

your local Agency on Aging listed in the blue section of your phone book. If you can't unearth the phone number, call ElderCare Locator at 800-677-1116 and they will find it for you.

GOVERNMENT LINKS TO DISCOUNTS

It doesn't have to be a program operated directly by the government to qualify for a government discount. Several other organizations offer discounted benefits to seniors. Two of the best are:

- State universities with dental schools. Many receive Uncle Sam's money for reduced-cost dental services, including regular care, dentures, implants, bridgework, and that ever-nasty root canal. For more information, call your state dental association, usually listed in your phone book under your state name, followed by "Dental Association" (for example, the Indiana Dental Association). You can also call the American Dental Association at 312-440-2593 for the location of a dental school near you.

- AARP (American Association of Retired

TOP SECRET

PRISONERS GET ANOTHER DAY IN COURT

Prisoners are suing both federal and state governments with enthusiasm. Taxpayer-paid lawsuits have been brought for such frivolities as bad haircuts by prison barbers, melted ice cream served in the mess hall, not enough salsa, too-tight prison-issue underwear, and improperly colored shower towels. One Minnesota prisoner said that his motive for suing was "pure delight in spending taxpayers' money."

Persons) offers some of the best and most diversified discounts anywhere for seniors. Dedicated to shaping and enriching the experience of aging, this association does receive federal funds for its member services, so tip your hat to the feds for the savings you'll receive if you join. If you are 50 or older, a membership fee of $8 per year (which also covers your spouse, who does not have to be 50 if *you* are) makes you eligible for discounts on airline tickets and airline vacation packages; car rentals; cruises; floral arrangements; hotels, motels, and resorts; online services including AOL, CompuServe, and Prodigy; prescriptions; and even a motoring plan that includes 24-hour roadside assistance and a personal travel planner.

For more information, check the AARP Web site at www.aarp.org. You may also contact AARP by phone at 800-424-3410 or write to: AARP, 601 E Street NW, Washington, DC 20049.

SEE THE USA

AMTRAK is government-funded. Thanks to those funds, those aged 62 or older can now receive a 15 percent discount on the

A BOOST FOR SENIOR ADVOCACY

In addition to arranging for travel, health, and business discounts for seniors and publishing "Modern Maturity," a magazine for those over 50, the American Association of Retired Persons (AARP) is at the forefront of political advocacy for seniors. Working from the belief that an informed citizen is a better citizen, AARP's Web site gives plenty of scrutiny to Uncle Sam and what he's up to. The AARP site allows you to see what Congress is discussing on any given day, shows you how to fire off e-mails to your representatives or senators, and provides guides to important legislation concerning seniors. Check it all out at www.aarp.org.

lowest fare to wherever they go (first-class tickets are *not* discounted, however). If you'd like a chance to ride the rails, check the Web site at www.amtrak.com or call 1-800-USA-RAIL.

IT'S GREAT TO BE GOLD

Of golden age, that is. For a one-time fee of $10, anyone 62 or over can buy the Golden Age Passport, which allows free access to most federal recreation areas and national parks and also gives a 50 percent discount on usage fees for camping and RV parking. Golden Age Passports can be purchased at any national park or federal recreation area. To contact the National Park Service for more information, see this web site: www.nps.gov. You may also call 202-208-6843 or write to: National Park Service, 1849 C Street NW, Washington, DC 20240.

If you are entitled to a discount for any product or service offered by the government, *ask for it.* It's your own money, after all.

GET FREE (YES, FREE!) GOODS FROM THE GOVERNMENT

Your Tax Dollars Pay for It Anyway

★ ★ ★ ★

THE GOVERNMENT TAKES, then takes some more. It's a fact of life. But the government does give a little, too. While you're not going to walk away with a lot of actual goodies in hand—no free cars, clothes, or chocolates—you *can* get tons of free information and advice that can make your life better. And worthwhile advice is almost as good as chocolate, isn't it?

THEY DO THE CRIME, YOU GET FREE MONEY

If you're in the right place at the right time, witnessing something you weren't meant to see, the government could have a reward for you if you. All these agencies authorize rewards for witnesses on a case-by-case basis.

- Is that mug shot in the post office really of your next-door neighbor? Find your local FBI office in the blue government pages of your phone book or call national headquarters at 800-688-9889.

- Did you witness a cruise employee emptying trash overboard? Videotape the deed or take pictures, then call the U.S. Coast Guard Marine Safety & Environmental

Protection Division at 202-267-2200.

- Do you suspect someone of dumping hazardous waste? Report them to the Criminal Investigations Division of the Environmental Protection Agency at 202-564-2557.

- Catch someone cheating on their taxes? Call the IRS at 800-829-1040.

- Did someone turn down the odometer mileage on that second-hand car you just bought? Call the Auto Safety Hotline at 800-424-9393.

- Is that Rolex a fake? If you remember where you bought it, call the U.S. Customs Service at 800-232-5378 (800-BE-ALERT).

FREEBIES FROM THE PREZ

Contrary to what you may think, the President *would* like to be included in a special event in your life. All you have to do is ask and he'll be there, in the form of an 8×10 photo and greetings honoring the following events:

1. Welcome baby! Send a birth announcement or write a note with the date of the child's birth.

2. Birthday greetings for those 80 and over.

3. A happy anniversary note for couples married 50 years or more.

4. A congratulatory note on your retirement.

5. A message of condolence.

Include as much information as you can for freebies 2 through 5 and send your request several months in advance to the White House Greetings Office, 1600 Pennsylvania Ave. NW, Washington, DC 20500.

WHY PAY MORE?

Taxes, that is. The U.S. Senate Special Committee on Aging has a sneaking hunch that many older Americans pay too much in taxes. Their report, "Protecting Older Americans Against Overpayment of Income Taxes," is available on the Web at www.senate.gov/~aging or by writing: Senate Special Committee on Aging, SD–G31 Dirksen Senate Building, Washington, DC 20510.

GOT THE TIME?

What happens when you have 12 clocks in your house and none show the same time? It's simple. For the cost of a phone call, you can access the Atomic Clock at the Naval Observatory for the exact time within milliseconds. Phone 202-762-1401.

HERE'S TO YOUR HEALTH

The government has a wealth of up-to-date health information waiting for you—if you know where to grab. Take a look at the National Institutes of Health Web site at www.nih.gov to get a feel for what's available, then contact the individual institutes for free information. Don't ask for treatment advice for that bunion on your big toe, though. Medical advice is not given.

- National Cancer Institute: Information on understanding, preventing, detecting, diagnosing, and treating cancer. Call 800-4-CANCER, TTY 800-332-8615. The Web site is www.nci.nih.gov.

- National Eye Institute: Conducts and supports research and training and disseminates information about eye disease. Call 301-496-5248, no TTY. The Web site is www.nei.nih.gov.

- National Heart, Lung and Blood Institute: Deals with diseases of the heart, blood vessels, and lungs. Call 301-592-8573, no TTY. The Web site is www.nhlbi.nih.gov.

- National Institute on Aging: Information on the social and behavioral aspects of aging, preventing age-related diseases, and promoting the quality of life of aging Americans. Call 800-222-2225, TTY 800-222-4225. The Web site is www.nih. gov/nia.

- National Institute on Alcohol Abuse and Alcoholism: Conducts research on improving treatment and prevention of alcoholism and alcohol-related problems. Call 301-443-3860, no TTY. The Web site is www.niaaa.nih.gov.

- National Institute of Allergy and Infectious Diseases: Information on understanding, treating, and preventing infectious, immunologic, and aller-

gic diseases. Call 301-496-5717, no TTY. Web site: www.niaid.nih.gov.

- National Institute of Diabetes and Digestive and Kidney Diseases: Information on diabetes, digestive, urologic, kidney, and hematologic diseases. Call 301-496-3583, no TTY. The Web site is www.niddk.nih.gov.

- National Institute on Drug Abuse: Deals with drug abuse, addiction, prevention, and treatment. Call 888-644-6432, TTY 888-889-6432. Web site: www.nida.nih.gov.

- National Institute of Neurological Disorders

WHO NEEDS TO BUY A COMPUTER?

Most of the information in this chapter has a Web site listed because computers are often the quickest way to get what you want. If you don't have a computer, *don't worry.* Most public libraries provide free computer time to patrons, and most librarians will be glad to help you get started if you're a complete computer novice. Just ask. Free computer time is also available at many university libraries, and some senior citizen centers have them, too. So check around. You don't need to invest a couple thousand bucks when you can get everything you need for free.

and Stroke: Information on the causes, prevention, diagnosis, and treatment of nervous system disorders including stroke, epilepsy, multiple sclerosis, Parkinson's disease, and Alzheimer's disease. Call 301-496-5751, no TTY. The Web address is www.ninds.nih.gov.

- National Institute of Mental Health: Dedicated to understanding, treating, and preventing mental illness. Call 301-443-3600, no TTY. The Web site is www.nimh.nih.gov.

- National Center for Complementary and Alternative Medicine: Identifies and evaluates unconventional health care practices. Call 888-644-6226. The TTY is the same number. The Web site is nccam.nih.gov (no "www").

- National Institute of Arthritis and Musculoskeletal and Skin Disorders: Conducts research on the normal structure and function of bones, muscles, and skin as well as diseases affecting these tissues. Call 301-495-4484, TTY 301-565-2966. The Web site is www.nih.gov/niams.

- National Institute on Deafness and Other Communication Disorders: Information on diseases and disorders of hearing, balance, smell, taste, voice, speech, and language. Call 800-241-1044, TTY 800-241-1055. Web site: www.nih.gov/nidcd.

- National Institute of Dental and Craniofacial Research: Deals with understanding, treating, and preventing infectious and inherited craniofacial, oral, and dental diseases. Call 301-402-7364, TTY 301-656-7581. Web sites: www.nidcr.nih.gov, www.nidr.nih.gov.

- National Institutes of Health Osteoporosis and Related Bone Diseases:

Information about osteoporosis and other serious diseases of the bone. Call 800-624-BONE, TTY 202-466-4315. The Web site is www.osteo.org.

OH, THE WEATHER OUTSIDE IS FRIGHTFUL . . .

And your house isn't keeping you warm. The Weatherization Assistance Program, sponsored by the Department of Energy, works to help low-income households receive cost-effective, energy-efficient improvements such as insulation, ventilation fans, and heating and cooling tune-ups. The Web site is www.eren.doe.gov. You can also call 202-586-4074 or write: U.S. Department of Energy, Office of State and Community Programs,

TOP SECRET

THREATS TO OUR SECURITY?

Protecting our country sometimes involves odd tactics. For some reason, the FBI kept a file on Spanish artist Pablo Picasso well into the 1990s, even though he had been dead for nearly 20 years.

Law enforcement is using strobe lights to make criminals disoriented and nauseous. Unfortunately, it has taken a little longer to develop the eye shields that immunize police officers from the dizzying light.

EE-44, 1000 Independence Ave. SW, Washington, DC 20585.

OH, THE WEATHER OUTSIDE IS FRIGHTFUL, AGAIN!

You may not want to find out much about natural disasters, but the Federal Emergency Management Agency (FEMA) has all you need to know about dealing with thunderstorms, tornadoes, tsunamis, and the like. Visit the FEMA Online Library at www.fema.gov/ library, then click on the "Preparedness and Training" section, or call 800-480-2520.

FINDING RELIEF FOR THAT FRIGHTFUL WEATHER

FEMA, in conjunction with the Small Business Administration and the Administration on Aging, offers financial assistance for seniors affected by a disaster. One form of aid is a low-interest, long-term loan. Another is a grant that doesn't have to be re-paid. Call FEMA at 800-462-9029, TTY 800-462-7585.

FREE EQUITY MONEY, ALMOST

If you need a little boost to your income, and you're 62 or older, you may be eligi-ble for a reverse mortgage. You can borrow against the equity in your house, but unlike traditional home equity loans, you won't be required to repay the loan

GIVE A LITTLE BIT BACK

Uncle Sam needs you. If you have the time, think about giving him some of it. Senior Corps has a variety of opportunities.

- Foster Grandparents (60 and over) devote their time to children with special or exceptional needs.

- Retired Senior and Volunteer Program (RSVP) provides hundreds of community services, from delivering meals to planning com-munity gardens. Please be 55 or over.

- Senior Companions (60 or older) reach out to adults who need some assistance to live independently.

For detailed information about the programs, visit the Web site at www.nationalservice.org. To find a Senior Corps program in your area, call 202-606-5000 (TTY 202-634-9256) or write: Corporation for National Service, 1201 New York Ave. NW, Washington, DC 20525.

until the house is no longer your primary residence. Call Housing and Urban Development at 888-466-3487.

CREDIT AND DIET AND CARS, OH MY!

Want the lowdown on water testing scams? Perhaps you'd like to know how to get those pesky telemarketers off your back. The Federal Trade Commission stands ready with free information and government warnings about these and dozens of other topics. Call 202-382-4357 (202-FTC-HELP) or visit their Web site at www.ftc.gov. You can also request a list of Consumer Protection publications from: Consumer Response Center, Federal Trade Commission, 600 Pennsylvania Ave. NW, Room H-130, Washington, DC 20580-0001.

GET THE SCOOP ON YOUR PRESCRIPTION DRUGS

Want to know more about that brand-new drug that your doctor prescribed? Check out the Food and Drug Administration web site at www.fda.gov. While you're there, browse some of the other options. You can get free information about food and cosmetics as well as consumer alerts. Information is also available by calling 888-463-6332 (888-INFO-FDA).

GET YOUR PRESCRIPTION DRUGS FREE

Dozens of pharmaceutical companies offer free prescription drugs to certain people who might not otherwise be able to get them. For a list of those companies, visit the Pharmaceutical Research and Manufacturers of America web site at www.phrma.org. Click on the "Publications" section and access the "Directory of Prescription Drug Patient Assistance Programs."

The PHRMA, a lobbying organization, is very active on Capitol Hill. They oppose limits on drug pricing,

TOP SECRET

WITH THIS KIND OF DEFENSE, WHO NEEDS AN ATTACK?

Following up on well-known overchargings such as hundred-dollar nuts and bolts and thousand-dollar toilet seats, Department of Defense contractors have more recently billed the government $260,000 for a Smokey Robinson concert, $20,194 for golf balls, $17,000 for the cost of hiring referees and umpires for office sports leagues, and $63,000 for crystal decanters awarded to top-performing employees.

fighting for higher costs for the purpose of R&D.

WITH A LITTLE HELP FROM SOME FRIENDS

One of the greatest creations since sliced bread is ElderCare Locator, a nationwide directory assistance service designed to help older persons and their caregivers locate local support resources. Your needs may be as simple as a daily meal or as complicated as home care, but ElderCare Locator will search for assistance free of charge and provide you with names and phone numbers of organizations in your area that can help. For more information, call 800-677-1116.

WHEN YOU NEED A PICTURE OF A RED—COCKADED WOODPECKER

The Fish and Wildlife Service now has a variety of images online. Most of them are in the public domain, which means they have no copyright restrictions and are free to use unless you see a specific reference to a copyright. You may use public domain images in print and electronic publications;

there's no fee to pay and no need to get permission for reusing them. Do give credit to the artist or the Fish and Wildlife Service, though. Images are available at info.fws.gov (no "www"). Click on "Photos/Images."

WANTED: PERRY MASON!

Well, you may not get Perry when you contact the Legal Services Corporation, but you *will* get the free legal advice you need. Established in 1974 by Congress, the LSC's mission is to give low-income Americans access to civil legal aid. The corporation itself will not offer legal advice but will locate an LSC program in your area that may be able to help. To locate your closest LSC participant, check the web site at www.lsc.gov. Click on "How to Get LSC's Help," call 202-336-8800, or write: Legal Services Corporation, 750 First St. NE, Tenth Floor, Washington, DC 20002-4250.

A WALK THROUGH HISTORY

Would you like to take a peek at the first draft of the Declaration of Independence in Jefferson's own handwriting, or the Emancipation Proclamation or Gettysburg Address in Lincoln's fine handwriting? Maybe you'd prefer to just sit back and read the accounts of an ex-slave or view an architectural retrospective of housing after World War II. The good news is, you don't have to go any farther than your computer to see the historic exhibits on display at the Library of Congress in Washington, DC. They're available to you, free of charge, at www.lcweb.loc.gov. Click on the "Exhibitions" icon and witness some of the events that have made this country great.

Finding free stuff from the government takes a little work, but you'll find it's worth the effort.

GOVERNMENT TRUTH IS STRANGER THAN FICTION

UFOs, Military Secrets, and Our Shrinking Defense

★ ★ ★ ★

IT IS EVIDENT FROM HISTORY that those in charge of our country haven't always been honest with us and haven't always run things efficiently or securely. From decades of lies about UFOs to ridiculous security breaches to government malfeasance, our recent history is dotted with moments most Americans wouldn't be too proud of.

UFO SECRETS

THEY KNEW IT ALL ALONG

Since 1947, the Air Force, through the Air Materiel Command division, has investigated UFOs and believed that sightings were real. However, political pressure from higher-ups in the government during the 1950s short-circuited the truth. Documents were falsified and destroyed and witnesses discredited in order to convince the public that nothing was "out there." The CIA now claims that years of UFO "cover-ups" were actually lies meant to conceal U-2 spy plane reconnaissance and testing.

WE KNOW THEY'RE OUT THERE

Eighty percent of Americans believe that the

government hides data on extraterrestrial life forms, and nine percent of us have either had contact with aliens or know someone who did. More people have reported seeing UFOs than voted for President Clinton in 1996. Thirty-one percent of those polled by Gallup believed that an actual alien craft crashed in the United States in 1947.

THANK YOU, MR. PRESIDENT

In 1969, then-governor of Georgia Jimmy Carter saw what he felt was a UFO. Later, as president, he pushed (unsuccessfully) for further UFO research.

THE TRUTH ABOUT UFOs?

All the dirt you need on extraterrestrials can be found where Mulder and Scully might never look—on the FBI's own web site (www. fbi.gov). The agency has quietly posted documents on the Net about reported unidentified flying objects, alleged alien abductions, and unexplained animal mutilation. Not surprisingly, most of these documents contain blacked-out passages and missing names.

NASA's ROLE

The scientists at the National Aeronautical and Space Administration (NASA) have made many efforts to contact extraterrestrial intelligence through the *Pioneer, Voyager,* and *TOPS* programs—but have so far, they say, been unsuccessful. Some individuals believe that NASA has knowledge of extraterrestrial intelligence and is covering it up.

UP FROM THE SKIES

U.S. astronauts have repeatedly seen UFOs on their missions. The UFOs seem to have continually monitored astronauts during their space missions, and most observers believe that NASA keeps this fact secret from the public. We can only speculate that astronauts have been sworn to secrecy regarding their UFO encounters.

ASTRONAUTS SPEAK UP

Two former U.S. astronauts have made their feelings known on UFOs, however. Gordon Cooper told the U.N. that he believed that extraterrestrial beings were visiting the Earth with advanced spacecraft, while Edgar Mitchell believes that extraterrestrials have crash-landed on Earth and that the U.S. government covers this up. He feels that our government has borrowed extraterrestrial technology and used it in its advanced military hardware.

DO YOU BELIEVE YOUR OWN EYES?

In July 1976, the *Viking* orbiter sent back images of Mars that appeared to look like a face. While NASA said that the "face on Mars" could be a shadow, or caused by erosion, wind, or other natural forces, some individuals were unconvinced by NASA's explanation and believe that it represents evidence of a long-lost Martian civiliza-

tion. Our Earth has few if any natural formations that look like faces. (Can you imagine aliens wondering about the faces on Mount Rushmore while their governments say that such formations are caused by shadow, erosion, wind, or natural forces?)

DOES THE GOVERNMENT KNOW THE TRUTH?

NASA certainly has demonstrated a keen interest in exploring the possibility of extraterrestrial life.

- In 1972, *Pioneer 10* was launched into outer space, carrying an aluminum plaque with a message to extraterrestrial civilizations. The message was designed to communicate the existence of Earth (and human beings) to any space intelligence that *Pioneer 10* might encounter.

- During the *Voyager 1* and *2* programs, NASA attached a phonograph record containing sounds and images selected to portray the diversity of life and culture on Earth to extraterrestrial civilizations. This seems like a lot of trouble and expense to go to just for the sake of a "fairy tale."

- In October 1992, Congress directed NASA to search for artificial radio signals from other civilizations. NASA created the Towards Other Planetary Systems (TOPS)/ High-Resolution Micro-wave Survey (HRMS) program to search for extraterrestrial radio signals. Congress ordered NASA to terminate the project in October 1993 before the program had detected any such signals.

- On August 6, 1996, a NASA research team found evidence that life may have existed on Mars 3.6 billion years ago. Organic molecules and other evidence of biological activity were found in a meteorite, thought to be of Martian origin, discovered in Antarctica in 1984. The meteorite fell to earth approximately 13,000 years ago.

ETs in WWII?

"Foo Fighters" were nicknames for the mysterious airplanes seen during World War II that failed to conform to the superpowers' known aerial technology of the time. These mysterious balls of light were reported by the experienced crews of American warplanes in both the European and Pacific Theaters in 1944–45. Foo Fighters, flying singly or in V-formations, were reported to have followed planes from both sides. Many theories were used to explain the cause of these phenomena, including the planet Venus, St. Elmo's Fire, or new enemy test weapons. It was assumed that the "other side" (the Allies or the Axis) had developed a secret weapon. However, after the war ended, it became clear that these fireballs weren't from *either* side.

FOO FIGHTERS IN FRANCE

In December 1942, while 7,000 feet over France, a Royal Air Force pilot saw two lights shooting from near the ground towards him. At first, he took the lights to be tracer fire from enemy positions. When the lights began to follow him, mimicking every evasive maneuver he made, the pilot realized the lights were under someone's control. The lights, which kept an even distance from each other, pursued him for several miles.

FOO FIGHTERS IN GERMANY

On September 29, 1944, at 10:45 A.M., a test pilot was trying out a new Messerschmitt jet when two luminous points to his right suddenly caught his attention. He shot full speed in that direction and found himself face-to-face with a cylindrical object more than 300 feet long. It had openings along its side and long antennae placed in front. Having approached within 1,500 feet of the craft, the pilot was amazed to see it moving at more than 1,200 mph.

DECIDE FOR YOURSELF

Want to see about UFOs for yourself? You now can access the National Archive's government UFO records—which run more than two million pages. Find out how to view copies of microfilm records from Project Blue Book and other UFO research projects by contacting the National Archives at www.nara.gov or calling 301-713-7250. You can also write to the following address: National Archives and Records Administration, Textual Reference Branch, 8601 Adelphi Road, College Park, MD 20740-6001.

MILITARY SECRETS

NO MORE SECRETS

Vice President Al Gore recently announced the

declassification and release of restricted Navy data about the world's oceans. In addition, the administration has ordered the Pentagon to produce computer-based nautical charts to replace the paper charts used by civilian mariners for centuries.

So what's the big deal? Well, it took the U.S. Navy a long time to become the greatest military force on the high seas. One great advantage of the United States' nuclear submarine fleet has been the data it has gathered over the years about ocean depths, which helped our ships hide under thermoclines (layers of water of varying temperatures). These data can change frequently and require constant updating. What permits the U.S. Navy to do that is better technology. Such information is now as open to the Chinese, Russians, and Iranians as it is to commercial interests, environmentalists, and scientists. Don't you feel safer now?

WHAT IS AT RISK?

The Navy is in the process of declassifying secret data from its Sound Surveillance System, an array of underwater listening devices used to hunt submarines. This acoustical data can also be used to track whale migrations, predict natural catastrophes, and support climate change research.

Does this mean the Navy views its mission to hunt enemy submarines as obsolete, or just of less importance than tracking whale migration?

"FRIENDLY" FIRE?

The U.S. government offered a $6,000 survivor benefit to one of the widows of a "friendly fire" serviceman killed in the F-15/Black Hawk helicopter incident in Northern Iraq. Meanwhile, 11 foreign citizens who died in the incident received $100,000 each.

The Navy is also releasing data on ocean temperature and salinity levels collected by submarines on patrol under the Arctic ice cap. Combined with declassified data from other oceans released by the Navy in recent years, the White House promises "this new information completes a global data set that will be a valuable tool in researching long-term climate change."

The Navy employs one of the nation's largest supercomputers to provide highly accurate, localized forecasts of battleground weather conditions. The Navy has now been ordered to work with the National Oceanic and Atmospheric Administration to share this highly sensitive and much-coveted know-how.

DUTCH HACKERS SELL OUR SECRETS TO SADDAM

A BBC–TV program claimed that hundreds of military secrets, including troop movements and missile capabilities, were stolen from U.S. Defense computers by Dutch cyberthieves and sold to Iraqi leader Saddam Hussein during the Gulf War. U.S. government officials watched as files on troop movements were accessed repeatedly by hackers originating from the Netherlands. Once the Dutch cyber-terrorists arrived at the correct systems, the TV program said, they fired salvos of IDs and passwords at the computers until access to the systems was granted.

OUR NATIONAL INSECURITY

LAX SECURITY EXPOSES SECRETS

Our government has been far from careful about safeguarding our military secrets against agents from other countries. China is the latest nation to benefit.

- One private American security guard for a U.S. satellite launch in China reported to duty carrying a sleeping bag.

- Another guard pushed a table out of view of

surveillance cameras and napped on it.

- Still others left windows unlocked, doors unsealed, and sensitive equipment and documents unguarded from Chinese technicians.

- Some came to work inebriated. Others consorted illegally with Chinese women.

- Irked by poor security, one U.S. official assigned to monitor a launch in China decided to test whether he could break into the satellite processing building. He got in and was able to sidle up to the security supervisor undetected.

Such security lapses are not isolated, according to a recent congressional report on Chinese espionage. They are, in fact, emblematic of a sometimes stunning lack of vigilance by U.S. government and industry in safeguarding weapons-related secrets from the agents of China's military modernization.

- Beijing mines information from between its estimated 3,000 corporations and 100,000 students and graduates in the U.S. as well as tens of thousands of delegation members who visit America each year. By tasking ordinary Chinese visitors—and, as needed, "sleeper" agents long established in the United States—with small, specific duties, Beijing's spy organizations can hide behind multiple fronts.

- "Sleeper" agent Bin Wu, a former Chinese philosophy professor, arrived in the U.S. after the 1989 Tiananmen protests. He set up several small front companies in Virginia. These companies sent U.S. technology to Chinese intelligence via Hong Kong. In 1993, he was convicted for smuggling third-generation night-vision equipment to China.